A LIFE ON FIRE

BILL FORD'S STORY

Co-written by Bill Ford and Steven Johns MA

Compiled by Steven Johns MA

Edited by Mary Johns

Illustrations by Richard Tilden Smith and Debbie Ford

Front Cover Illustration by Ian Ward

Photographs by Graham Wignall

Graphic Design by Alison Poole Designs Ltd

www.alifeonfire.co.uk

This first edition published 1st May 2018
by
A Life on Fire Limited
1 Burton Road
Sileby
Loughborough
Leicestershire
LE12 7RU

Email: info@alifeonfire.co.uk
www,alifeonfire.co.uk

Graphic Design by Alison Poole Designs Limited
10 Priory Drive, Stainton, Middlesbrough TS8 9AW
www.alisonpooledesigns.co.uk

Public Relations and Marketing by
Kate Tilley at Dream Big Marketing
kate@dreambigmarketing.co.uk

Print and print management by
Biddles
Castle House, East Winch Road, Blackborough End, Kings Lynn, Norfolk PE32 1SF
United Kingdom

ISBN 978-1-9996345-9-9

Typeset in Plantin Light

For Debbie, Kerry, Jane, Ian and Julia

Contents

Foreword by Nicky Morgan MP

I first met Bill Ford in 2009 when I asked if I, and the then Shadow Minister for Transport, could visit the Great Central Railway in Loughborough. Bill spent several hours with us and took us not only to Quorn on a steam train in a luxury directors carriage but treated us to lunch. This was to be the beginning of our working relationship as I became Loughborough's MP and then one of the founding members and first Chairman of the All Party Parliamentary Group on Heritage Rail.

When we meet someone we meet them at that point in their history. In Bill's case he was Managing Director of the Great Central Railway and I had no knowledge of the industrialist and businessman he had been and which this book captures.

Little by little, amidst trips on the railway, meetings at Lovatt House and breakfasts in Loughborough, I began to find out just how lucky the GCR had been to secure Bill's support at a critical moment in their history. Bill is someone who knows how to attract investment and keep investors happy and how to juggle multiple competing interests and demands which can require nerves of steel.

Over the years I came to know that Bill wasn't just someone

who talked a good game but someone who worked incredibly hard, using his extensive business experience, to turn a railway severely down on its luck into the Great Central Railway we have today with its beloved Santa Trains, 1940s weekend, busy cafes and popular steam and diesel weekends.

Bill would talk to anyone and everyone to get GCR projects off the ground. Like so many business people he got frustrated by red tape and bureaucracy. But he knew how to win over supporters and make people feel special. He always wanted everything to go further and faster – of course, trains and drivers responded better to that pressure than local and national government, especially the planners, much to his annoyance!

Once the formalities of an event were over he then wanted to get on with enjoying the railway and watching the pleasure it gave to the many thousands of people who visit each year. He was always very proud of how many visitors had attended each special event.

The greatest project, which remains to be completed but which has come a long way because of his drive and vision, is the re-unification of the railways and the re-building of the bridge over the Midland Main Line. This has been a huge team effort but Bill was always there in the middle of the planning refusing to take 'no' for an answer. The sense of genuine excitement and wonder, amongst the grown-ups never mind the young railway enthusiasts, as the bridge was lifted into place in 2017 was a testament to how important this project is to the railway and its long-standing and dedicated members and supporters.

It is too easy to dismiss GCR employees, volunteers and supporters as amateur heritage railway enthusiasts and miss the fact that they are now running a thriving business and tourist attraction whose success is vitally important to the economic story of our corner of Leicestershire. The fact that transformation happened is due, in large part, to the enormous contribution made to the Great Central Railway's history by Bill Ford. His story deserves to be told.

★　　★　　★

Introduction by Steven Johns

If you Google "Bill Ford" you get a lot of American suggestions and references to automobiles. Inevitable with a surname like that I suppose, but a more British man you could not wish to meet. Meeting him for the first time, you feel you already know him; he engages with you, doesn't threaten or pry, but listens to what you have to say and understands. He has a quiet authority that deserves respect rather than demands it; some who rise to lofty management levels lack this trait, leading by rule and regulation with loud or aggressive threats and sanctions. They tend not to last though.

I first met Bill Ford officially on November 3rd 2014 in his office at Lovatt House whilst I was a volunteer with The Great Central Railway in Loughborough, Leicestershire. Bill was a volunteer too, and by that I mean unwaged, but he was a shareholder and managing director of the charity PLC which ran the heritage GCR from Loughborough to Birstall near Leicester. On his desk, which was more like a boardroom table, was a five foot precision engineered model of the now preserved Jubilee Class railway locomotive Leander. The original loco, built a year before Bill was born, had once been half owned by him until a few years previously. What a memento!

I'd been asked to join the editorial team of MainLine - the quarterly magazine that reports on all things happening at the

9

GCR. I think the relationship between Bill and the then current editor had become a little strained and a stop gap may have been required if the strain got any worse; but things improved and with a bit of my help the magazine flourished. It now has a new editor and the Great Central has a new board of directors.

The autumn and winter of 2014 had been a momentous time for the GCR: there were two bids in place for Lottery funding for projects that were hardly but a pipe dream a decade earlier. The first and foremost was to replace the bridge over the Midland Main Line that had been removed in the 1960s after the infamous Beeching axe had closed the railway. This bridge would join up two preserved sections of the railway to give a continuous steam-hauled Main Line run from just south of Nottingham to just north of Leicester. The second project was the proposal to build a museum at the Leicester end of the line, thus creating the first live steam museum in the UK and making the GCR an official affiliate part of the National Railway Museum. Bill showed me the artists' impressions and architects' drawings of the plans.

Following the progress of the railway's fortunes, from Bill's letters published in each MainLine magazine, it was obvious what a gigantic juggling act keeping everything together actually was. Year on year the struggle for cash had continued; the railway had never made an operating profit in more than

40 years since the formation of the entity as a heritage railway. Every year it ran at a loss and the directors would have to go cap in hand to sponsors and benefactors to make up that loss. Add to this the dilapidated infrastructure, with everything from signals and signs, canopies and carriages, buildings, boilers and benches disintegrating almost before your eyes, which mostly weren't part of the operating losses and all needing funds to maintain, and it is amazing to find that the GCR exists at all. Without the work and dedication of hundreds of volunteers it wouldn't exist anyway, but substantial funds are always required and that money flow needs to be managed properly. It is also important to factor in the perilous state the company has been in on several occasions over the years, within minutes of bankruptcy at times, with banks withdrawing overdrafts and on one occasion actually having to have a whip round of all the senior staff and senior volunteers so that a monthly wage bill could be paid. With every issue of MainLine the story of the struggle unfolded through Bill's letters, but there was always the infectious enthusiasm and faith shining through his words that if we all pull together the GCR will move forward to achieve greater things.

In 2009 the operating turnover of the Railway was £1.25 million with the loss about 10% of that. January 2017's annual accounts for the PLC show that turnover had risen to more than twice that with an operating profit for the first time.

There are many facets to the founding, existence, survival and eventual success of all manner of enterprises, but it is more often than not a single element that proves paramount as to the reason it is there at all. You can use analogies to describe the GCR – like the house of cards, when you remove one it all falls down, or the motor car with a wheel missing that will not run - but it is my firm belief that without Bill Ford and his unwavering guidance, intuition, financial acumen, business experience, people skills and can-do/will-do attitude, the railway and all its resources would exist only as history. The land it occupies would have been sold for house building, the engines housed in museums or scrapped, carriages and wagons lost in the weed infested sidings of yesteryear and a thousand volunteers would be without a purpose.

Bill's letter in the summer 2016 edition of MainLine foretold the changes required on the board of directors at the GCR. These were necessary to cope with the retirement of some directors and the addition of others to improve the accountability required when dealing with large projects and substantial sums of public money from lottery funding. It's important to note that there would have been no lottery funding had the railway not been on course to survive and prosper. Bill had intimated for some time that he'd like to take a less intense role and make way for a younger person to steer the company into the new era. At a board meeting in October

2016, where Bill was absent due to ill health, the new board was elected and Bill's managerial association and involvement with the Great Central Railway was ended. There was no ceremony, no "wish you well", nothing. The writing was firmly on the wall. He was asked to leave his office with immediate effect. The new CEO even asked if he would like to donate his precious Leander to the museum!

This was the beginning of my discovery of the life and times of William John Charles Ford. He's an octogenarian and like Leander, he requires a bit of maintenance and repair now and therefore shouldn't have to pull too much weight too often. Like us all, and preserved steam loco's too, he'll continue to thrive with a good deal of T.L.C. and I bet this is not the end of either of their Main Line days.

Accompany me now to the start of this journey of more than three and a half million miles. We'll travel to every continent on earth; do business with companies with household names and with directors in Africa, Sheiks in Arabia and Mayors in Leicester, politicians in Westminster and councillors in Charnwood. We'll fly aeroplanes over the top of Kilimanjaro, join the Mile High Club, buy and sell trucks from Lord Stokes, a railway from British Railways and become friends with Lord Lanesborough. We'll cruise on Her Majesty's ocean liners to Cape Town and drive legally at over a hundred and eighty miles per hour on English roads in Ferraris, Aston Martins, E Type Jaguars and Austin Healeys; we'll travel sedately in Rolls Royces, Bentleys, narrow boats and more. We'll make and spend millions of pounds along the way, become a tax exile in the Isle of Man, live in halls and manors in splendid countryside and bachelor pads in London. We'll share his faith in people, Christian Science and his family. We'll see how he avoids the clutches of the grim reaper in war, disease and tragic accident so that he survives to tell his tale of A Life on Fire...

★ ★ ★

Introduction by Bill Ford

Many times throughout my life, friends family and associates have urged me to write my story.

"You must write your book!" they'd say...

It wasn't until the autumn of 2016, in the autumn of my life, that I found the time, the space, the motivation and the reason to tell my story.

"Yeah, yeah," I'd say, and then get on with what it was I was running, saving, growing, managing or whatever.

Until about three years ago, I never thought about how old I was and I certainly didn't feel I was anywhere near eighty years old. Then, for some reason - perhaps it was the death of a friend, or another health scare - I began to consider my life, my story, in earnest.

This gives me the opportunity to show you what life was like back in the 50s and 60s in colonial East Africa, where and when I worked there, and what could be achieved – much of it impossible today. In my mid-twenties we could finish work in Nairobi on Friday, drive three hundred miles in six hours to a party in Mombasa or Malindi, on what was nothing more than dirt roads, spend Saturday and most of Sunday partying, then drive back ready for work first thing on Monday. It would take two days one way these days, because the roads have been left unmaintained.

The last time I visited Dar es Salaam in Tanzania was in 1988. I took my family there for a holiday whilst I was working in Jeddah. In the early 1960s, when I worked for Lord Stokes at British Leyland, it was a beautiful place – it took your breath away. Living there was a dream. In 1988 so much had changed. Law and order had broken down, the streets were dirty, decay was all around, the city and the country was bankrupt. I cried. Colonialism provided progress, order and managed wealth properly. That wealth largely stayed in the country and with the people. Now, the money finds its way to the leaders and stays there, whilst the nations rot. There's enormous wealth out there, but there's no one to organise or manage it, or any will to distribute it fairly. It's a way of life that is now lost, probably forever.

Life, everywhere, has become more aggressive. "What's in it for me" is the common cry these days.

I understand that memory can be selective depending upon ones disposition, whether you view your lot in a positive way or not, but I have seen the world change dramatically in my life, and I do mean the world at large. I am in a position to comment, I believe, having worked and lived in a large part of it, and I have certainly travelled and done business throughout the world many times over. What I aim to achieve with this book is to record the amazing world I prospered in, to examine why I succeeded and others didn't, where I failed and the reasons why. I'll give you a glimpse into the lives of the people I have worked and lived with, many were good, honest and hardworking, some were chancers and some were crooks. Some were good crooks and some were bad.

I have been a busy person all my life, at least as far in my past as I can recall. I believe I became like this as a result of my Father; not because he was a busy person per se, but because he didn't like lazy people, and whenever I was around him it was vital for me to be busy. I am by nature a very lazy person and perhaps a therapist might suggest that my busy-ness is merely displacement activity. That is also, I believe, why I am a master at team building and delegating – once you have the right people in the right place, my work is then mostly done and I can get on with other stuff…

I can remember right back to the fourteenth night of November 1940. I was wearing a sky blue siren suit, the forerunner of the onesie and the boiler suit. My mother had carried little me, not quite three years old, down into the Anderson shelter where the floor had a foot of water in it, in the garden of our home at 18 Marina Road, Evington, Leicester. Looking back on my life, it seems I have never strayed too far from a work place populated by workers wearing boiler suits.

I still hear the sirens wailing when I think back to those times. As the sirens died, at half time as it were, and the first raid was over, my mother, in her soft Scottish accent would ask

"Anyone like a cup of tea?" And up she'd go with her usual courage leaving the men sitting around in the shelter.

I didn't see the bombs falling but I saw the havoc they wreaked. It was the night Coventry was first bombed in the war, and a few stray Luftwaffe bombers mistook Leicester for Coventry. A few days afterwards I was taken by Jim Scott who worked for my father's firm as our petrol pump attendant and delivery driver to deliver a Vulcan lorry to Coventry. We couldn't get to our destination. Many of the roads had been turned into bomb craters and there was no way through. House after house and street after street were just rubble. And fires were still burning. Memories like that never fade.

Now, as I assemble my memories with the help of fellow GCR volunteers Richard Tilden Smith and Steven Johns I find myself facing a continuous run of empty pages in my diary, probably for the first time in my life since I left school. And, I have to admit it scares me half to death; that laziness will creep back in and surely throttle the life from me.

Most of us would hope to be taking things a bit easier after four score years and would perhaps relish a good few empty diary pages, so that we could relax and slow down a bit. But it fills me with a kind of dread I suppose; posing questions from within such as, "Am I on the scrap heap?"

I've been running things and in control for so long, perhaps I've lost the ability to let life just flow. I could analyse the reasons for where I find myself right now until the end of my life, and still not understand the why and wherefore. But my upbringing, pedigree, religion, spirituality and common sense bids me to leave it alone and move on. What it has done is to give me the necessary time to concentrate and the incentive to write my book.

I'll give my account of my time with the GCR at the end of my book and you can make your own mind up about all that transpired there at that point. But I would ask that you read my entire story, as I present it here, so that you have the context and the background to my whole life.

★   ★   ★

"Beauty is truth, truth beauty,
That is all ye know on earth,
And all ye need to know"
                    Keats

Hand written in June 1955 by school friend Graham
Arkell to me in the book of hymns and carols entitled
"Cantata Stoica" which is given to each boy when he
begins his education at Stowe school.

Part One

England, pre1937 - 1960

My earliest memory is of the night Coventry was bombed. I can remember my mother holding me at the entrance of our Anderson Shelter as the Luftwaffe bombers flew overhead. The Germans mistook Leicester for Coventry...

18 Marina Road, Evington Leicester 1937

We receive 23 chromosomes from our mother and 23 from our

father. These carry our entire DNA, our genes, the building blocks

of who we are.

Richard Dawkins – The Selfish Gene

Chapter 1

From Whence I came

My mother was a hundred percent Scottish, from a line recorded back to The Clan McRoberts of Tarland, in the Cambrian Mountains, Aberdeenshire in the 17th century. The family were also closely connected to the Gordon clan in Aberdeenshire.

Her most famous relative was General Gordon of Khartoum who was her great, great uncle. Amongst his accolades was that he travelled almost as much as I did in his life, although his triumphs, victories and commands were rather more notable and historic than my own. But perhaps that I have lived longer than him is compensation enough.

My mother's family, the Kynochs, moved to Loughborough from near to Edinburgh after the First World War. She never lost her soft Scottish accent, and I am often reminded of her when I hear a similar dialect on the radio or the TV; some female presenters speak the same. It is a gift they have, perfect diction and phrasing and there's a smile in every sentence if you know what I mean, but perhaps I am biased. Although, to me she was Mother and her accent I only noticed when I listened to her recorded voice.

The Kynoch family, according to family folklore, had a "bit of a reputation" in and around Loughborough, although I have never been privy to any details.

My father's family were of Irish ancestry and had no one of recorded historic note in the line. Although, my father was born in 1902 on the Stapleford Park estate, home of the Lord Lieutenant of Leicestershire, the Kings representative in our county. My grandfather was the game keeper there and the Ford family had held a gamekeeper's position for 200 years. But Father didn't want to follow in the family trade and left school at the age of 14 to work on the railways. My father's brother, Ken, became a Christian Scientist before the Second World War, my father and Tom Slater following thereafter.

The religion you are born into is often a powerful and character forming influence, as it has been for me; why they changed from Church of England in my father's generation is still a mystery – I have never questioned it.

Father got into the motor industry in 1917 having left the railway at the age of 15. He worked for Bachelor Bowles along with Tom Slater who was an electrician. My father's brother, Ken, joined the company a little later and by the age of twenty one was promoted to foreman. Bachelor Bowles were the main agents in Leicestershire for General Motors dealing in American trucks and cars. They continued to work for Frank Bowles until, in 1928 two years after the general strike when recession was still a major problem, they decided to leave Bachelor Bowles and start their own business in small premises in a side street called Stonebridge Street, near

Spinney Hill Park.

My father's brother, Ken, joined them in 1930. Ford and Slater were able to move to much larger premises in Gwendolen Road Evington, through the friendship of Bill Cuffin.

Father met my mother and they married in 1932, moving to a modest 3 bedroomed, semi-detached property in Evington. My sister Jacqueline was born on July 2nd 1933, the same birthday as my father. She was two months premature, a blue baby and wrapped in cotton wool for the first three months of her existence. She finally grew to five foot eight and twelve stone after the birth of her second child.

Life in the thirties was very traditional by today's standards. Mothers kept the home and fathers earned the wages. Back then, the harder you worked, the smarter you were and the more diligent and honest your business was, the more you earned. My father, Tom Slater and Uncle Ken were perfect partners, and during the 1930s this was enhanced when all three of them joining the Christian Science Movement. Their shared Christian ethics, common sense and attention to detail assured them of a steadfast and secure business. Father always had an eye open for opportunities, a gift he has surely passed on to me.

Imagine those days for a moment or two. The internal combustion engine was just coming of age and anyone who learned its ways and knew how to maintain and harness the development and advancement was always going to do well in that world. The Fords and Slaters were in the right place at the right time. Rail was still the transport king, but because freight and people could only travel from railhead to railhead and commerce and people movement was growing exponentially, there was a massive growing demand to move those people and those goods from the railheads and stations into the communities. Trucks, vans, lorries and buses were needed in thousands to serve every city and town. In Leicestershire alone in 1935 there were over 70 railway stations with at least one serving every village or parish. Each day there were more than 1,700 trains stopping at these stations loading and unloading people and goods, with every train met by a taxi, bus, van or lorry. All these taxis, vans, buses and lorries needed regular maintenance and fuel. It's easy to see, that with hard work charged out at a fair price a business would prosper in such conditions. Prosper they did, but they ploughed all of that prosperity back into the business and even by the mid 1950s they only paid themselves an average working wage.

So, it is at this point in time I begin my life. I don't see myself as born with a silver spoon in my mouth, more of a chromium plated greasy torque wrench perhaps. But I do confess that I was lucky to be born into a family with a heritage where hard work provided for a good life, even in austere times as they were during and after the war.

Ford & Slater
Stonebridge St, Leicester?

LES

Stonebridge Street garage where Ford and Slater began in 1928

"Luckily, life is not so easy as all that; otherwise we should get to the end too quickly..."

Winston Churchill - My Early Life

Chapter 2

The First Time I Got My Cards

My entry into conscious life, through the fire, flood and bomb shelter of the Blitz, and the austere times I was born into with a nation at war, I took for granted and it certainly colours my recollections. This has no doubt influenced the choices, predicaments and direction that my life has taken. However, those pages of my memory are not grey, misty, out-of-focus and rubble-strewn - more a scrapbook of bright adventures connected, it seems, at junctions by massive personal changes. What ultimate wisdom will emerge from this remembering and writing process is yet to unfold, but already I detect a pattern is forming: life changing events throw one forward into new challenges, opportunities and sometimes follies.

Father worked seven days a week, but work for him, and me, often by his side in those pre-school days, seemed always to be an adventure. For me it was unfettered joy. And, many times, work involved me travelling with him on the passenger seat of his Morris Eight on some urgent errand or other. These were the days of rationing, with everything in short supply, unless you had something more precious than food to barter with. A cry for help from a farmer to fix a broken down motor vehicle often came with a dozen fresh eggs or rashers of bacon. And, of course, we had liquid gold as part of our stock in trade.

One of our weekly runs was to George Waite at Broughton Lodge, on the A46 between Leicester and Nottingham. Today, on the site of George Waite's old farm, stands the Best Western Leicester North Hotel next to the Go Kart centre. Dad would exchange a two gallon can of petrol for three dozen eggs.

On one occasion, as we were turning onto the Melton Road to come back to Leicester, we were stopped by a policeman. Bear in mind that official vendors supplying rationed goods without coupons was a serious offence in those early days of the war and, if caught, imprisonment could well be the outcome for perpetrators. It was too late to hide the eggs which were on the back seat. The policeman peered into my window which was open, and with a knowing grin said something along the lines of, "What have we here then?" At the officer's side was an airman, a flight lieutenant, I believe. The policeman, after glancing in the back of the car, asked if we could take the airman to Leicester Midland station as he had a train to catch back to his base. In wartime you could not refuse such a request from a police officer.

Father said, "Certainly officer, and is there anything else we can do to help?"

"No, that will be all," said the policeman, opening the door for the airman and adding with a knowing grin, "And mind those eggs!"

For the rest of my father's life and for mine too, we were never sure if the policeman had known the eggs were procured illegally or whether he just meant us to take care.

G. W. Waite was an extremely interesting individual. He started his working life at the Humber Cycle and Motor Company in the late 19th century. There, in 1888, he introduced what was probably the very first armed road vehicle. This was not a lorry, bus, car or even a motorcycle but a pedal cycle. In the 1880s various armed forces were experimenting with units of armed cyclists and these were not as ridiculous as might at first seem to be the case. These troops fulfilled a similar role to that of mounted infantry, fighting on foot but using their mounts for relatively rapid transit to the scene of action. A bicycle has some advantages over a horse when used in this role, for it is unnecessary to reserve men to be horse holders whilst their comrades engage the enemy. A mounted infantry unit could lose up to ten percent of its firepower as men were detailed for this task. Nor do cycles need supplies of fodder, as a substantial part of the supply train of an army at that time was devoted to carrying food for horses. Neither do they need to be supported by farriers and vets - although they might need some mechanics. In general most bicycles are more docile than a horse and it is usually quicker to teach a man to ride a bike than a quadruped!

Alas, George's invention never caught on, probably due to the rapid advancement of the internal combustion engine, but it did spur him on to form and build the only Leicester city company ever to design and manufacture cycles, motorcycles and cars.

In those days George Waite needed Father's petrol to run one of only three remaining cars built by him – the 1906 veteran Clyde motor car, which he named 'The Old Grey Mare'. Even into his late eighties he was writing 7 year plans - perhaps that's where I got it from - and the poor chap only died because he fell down the stairs at Broughton Lodge in the 1950s.

Before I started at school, most days I'd walk with Father the quarter of a mile to work from Marina Road to Gwendolen Road, and we'd always arrive for 8 am. I did feel like part of the workforce; I was paid the princely sum of a shilling a week and payday was on Fridays, the same time as everyone else. I was "apprenticed" to a WW1 veteran called Bert, who then would have been in his seventies. His job was to strip down Perkins diesel engines that had come from their works in Peterborough. Ford and Slater had a major contract with them. Bert and I would replace worn out parts and rebuild the engines. Bert sat on an old truck seat with me on a little stool beside him. That was where and when I learned the first rudiments of how an engine works and Bert used to tell me, "You'll be an engine engineer one day!".

I don't think Tom Slater, Father's business partner, thought much of me back then, if ever the truth be known! Although, on balance, he was not one to profess much about anything. He was a very hard worker and a very modest man in his tastes and outlook. It is notable that Tom never married and when he died he left all his money to the Church of Christian Science, which would have been a considerable fortune in 1986. If I were unkind I'd have to call him gruff, with a sharp tongue, stingy and a bit of a skin flint; after all, he was a Yorkshireman!

Something happened to him in his upbringing that he never shared with anyone else, and it was this, I guess, that influenced him to seek answers with religion and the Christian Science movement. It was Tom who introduced my father to Christian Science. I was once told by a Christian teacher that following your church's teachings makes you a better person. It rounds off rough edges, mellows an angry temper, and makes a selfish man generous. All I can say is, I am very pleased I never knew Tom Slater before he had found his religion!

These days a three or four year old wouldn't be allowed anywhere near such a dangerous place and an owner would probably be jailed if anything happened as did happen to me one day. I was "helping" a mechanic underneath the chassis of a Vulcan truck and gouged my head on the chassis frame. I had to go to hospital to have it stitched up and I was made to stay at home for a couple of days. I still have the scar to this day.

Some time after this incident, on a Friday that Father had to go out, it was my Uncle Ken who brought round the wages. I think Tom had made up the wage packets because in mine there was only sixpence instead of the expected shilling. He said it was because I had had time off and therefore I wasn't due any more. I was so angry that I asked for my cards there and then. I didn't even know what my cards were exactly and I certainly didn't know the consequences of demanding them. I suppose I had heard the men have arguments with Father and Tom and this was the threat that seemed to resolve things. But Tom and Ken called my bluff, brought them to me, and I walked home on my own. I bet I muttered some un-Christian words on my way!

I think now, though, it was a plan hatched up by the three of them, because it was time I was off their hands.

Looking back on those pre-school days, I suppose I was becoming a bit of a liability and it was always planned to send me to school as soon as it was possible. I was also probably becoming a bit of a handful at work with Father. But toys were not abundant then so we made our own fun, or mischief, or 'went to work' until you were old enough to attend school.

As happens so often, change means life will never be the same again. In my life there was never any gradual metamorphosis, more of a lurch into an abyss where I burned and failed or learned and grew. But, you will come to realise as you read on, as I do myself as I write this book, that most change was of my own unwitting making.

★   ★   ★

"Dr. Thomas Arnold: A new boy is always important. He may be an influence for good or for evil."

Thomas Hughes - Tom Brown's Schooldays

Chapter 3

School days

So then, as a four year old, I started my traditional education at Rowsley Street. My sister was already attending the same school and she walked the one and a half miles with me each day, gas masks in hand.

Rowsley Street was a private school run by the two Miss Grimleys, state education not beginning until a child reached five years of age. If my sister had to stay on after school for games or whatever, I remember our home help, a Miss Maycock who lived with her sister, would walk home with me. I stayed at Rowsley Street until I was five and could attend a junior preparatory school. Quite soon I was teaching incoming kids the alphabet and I have always been pretty good at English language and grammar ever since.

I had learned how to let car tyres down and one lunch time when Father came home, I let his tyres down; I never told him it was me until he was much older. It was one of those naughty things, a dark secret that burdens our conscience now and again. I did tell him towards the end of his life what I had done, and I probably would have felt relieved to get it off my chest had he not been so massively cross. That's a secret I should have kept to myself, or from him at least.

As soon as I was five I was sent to Stoneygate College as a boarder. There were three boys and nine girls boarding and the rest were day school students. I wasn't happy there. I learned some things I am sure and those things are an integral part of who I have become, part of the fabric of me, but most of my knowledge gained then wasn't academic at all.

I still find it curious that my parents sent me just a mile away to Stoneygate in Leicester as a boarder, although I did come home at weekends and holidays. Perhaps Father *did* know about the deflated tyres, and that was my punishment? But, if that were so, why was he so cross with me for owning up all those years later? That's one that will have to remain a mystery. In the words of that excellent song by Mike and the Mechanics "I wish I could have asked him... in the living years."

On Monday, 4th December 1944, my seventh birthday, I was expelled from Stoneygate College for starting a fire in the school dormitory. I was fascinated with matches for some reason that now completely escapes me. It wasn't a bad fire, just a few bits of rag and paper behind a movable wardrobe. The plywood back burned quite well and also set fire to the paint on the skirting board. I did put it out again shortly afterwards, as I had planned to do, but that fact was not taken into consideration at all. From today's perspective my punishment is more understandable as smoke from the burning paint and plywood enveloped the dormitories. I never liked the frosty old headmistress, Miss Knight, and she never liked me either. Her parting threats to me and my father were, "That boy will end up swinging on the end of a rope!" and "I will make sure he never gets into another school in Leicestershire!"

From that day on until hanging was abolished in 1965 I lived in dread of Miss Knight's statement coming true. However, whilst I considered setting a school on fire to be reasonable in the circumstances, killing somebody never crossed my mind.

Until the last week of January 1945 I didn't get into another school anywhere, I was blissfully pleased to find. I remember it was the most wonderful Christmas I'd ever had. A guilty conscience had not reared its fearsome head at that time.

My Uncle Frank Kynoch had previously bought me a second hand Meccano set and I loved the designing and building process. Of course, as every Meccano enthusiast throughout the ages will understand, compromise is the only way to succeed. No matter how many pieces you have, there's always a bit missing that you have to find a way around so you can complete the model. The most ambitious structure I ever attempted was the Eiffel Tower. I ran out of pieces when it was nearly finished and I needed gears to connect the clockwork motors, but I was very proud of it as it looked just like one of the pictures I'd seen in a book showing the stages of its construction in the 1880s.

So Christmas 1944 is a blissful memory for me. And it was made better because, as far as I knew, there'd be no more school and certainly no more crabby Miss Knight with whom to contend. Looking back from today's state of abundance, one feels that life in the war years must have been hard. But it's all a matter of relativity, not in the Einsteinian sense, but in that if you've never had it you'll never miss it and at the age of seven you can say for certain that I hadn't had much at all.

On Christmas morning when my sister and I awoke, there'd be a red and white knitted stocking Mother had made hanging on the end of our beds. This was filled with a bag of nuts, two oranges, a banana and an assortment of candies and sweets. I carried on this most enjoyable of traditions with my own children and they with their own, I guess. We both had three presents each which were hand made toys made by Mother. I had a large 3 mast ship with my other two presents on the deck of the ship - I have forgotten what they were.

Father took advantage of his ability to barter with his contacts, especially after the exchange scheme came into being when it became legal to swap rationed goods for other rationed goods. The local sweet shop owner swapped bags of toffees for work on his van, a grocer swapped mincemeat, flour and sugar for petrol and so on.

Mother, being a farmer's daughter, could 'compromise' the most delicious fare out of very humble ingredients. We had mince pies, pork pies and Christmas puddings with silver three-penny pieces in them; there was plenty to go around and then some. Chicken dinner came with all the trimmings: little sausages, bright orange carrots, green vegetables, creamy, steamy potatoes and rich dark brown gravy.

'Uncle' Tom came for Christmas dinner, stayed to enjoy the afternoon with us all and to listen to Winston Churchill and King George on the radio.

Christmas ended that year on January 22nd...

About a mile away from Stoneygate College was Stoneygate School, connected in name and proximity only as both schools were in the Stoneygate area of the city of Leicester. It was a day school so there were no boarders and I could come home every evening. A veteran World War One sea captain ran the school: a certain Captain Rudd. Father had been to see him in the run up to Christmas, told him of our predicament and Captain Rudd had said, "I like a lad with a bit of spirit!" Another veteran sea captain was my form teacher, Captain Cook, and lads with spirit were dealt with summarily with six of the best. He'd demand that you bend over and if you didn't bend over far enough he'd yell, "No boy, more like an egg! Touch your toes!"

One day I refused. I was then sent to Captain Rudd. My spirit was diluted somewhat thereafter. Even though I was not a very well behaved boy then, word of my delinquency never reached home, or so I thought. I was conversing with Mother and Father one day, telling them how a boy had been caned for some heinous crime or other, when I remarked, "You could see the dust come out his trousers the master hit him so hard."

"And does the dust come out of your trousers, Billy?" Mother asked.

Caught off guard, I replied, "I suppose so..."

Mothers make excellent detectives don't you think?

My best friend at Stoneygate School was a boy called Malcolm Higham who spoke with what I considered to be a rather over posh accent. He'd say barth for bath, and larf for laugh. But it was because he was a Cockney and I found out years later that he became a Pearly King in Hackney. Pearly Kings and Queens, known as Pearlies, are now an organised charitable tradition of working class culture and are honoured with an inherited title as Pearly King or Pearly Queen of a borough of London. The association was originally formed by Henry Croft in the 1880s who was a street seller of vegetables, a costermonger, in the East End of London. They would sow hundreds of mother of pearl buttons onto their jackets and trousers to brighten up their attire, hence they became known as Pearlies. The association came into being as a result of fellow costermongers falling upon hard times, and Henry Croft would organise a 'whip round' to help them back on their feet. Today they raise hundreds of thousands of pounds for local charities and good causes.

My parents always thought it was Malcolm who led me astray because he was a couple of years my senior. But really we were both as bad as each other. Malcolm came from a long line of street sellers and I suppose scrumping was in his DNA. He and I were as thick as thieves - well we were thieves actually, although I wasn't aware of what crime was back then. I recall proudly showing Mother what I had acquired after a Saturday foray into Woolworths. Malcolm had showed me the ropes and because he was older and so confident in getting away with it I thought it must be alright. We weren't greedy, we each took two or three little things from the toy counter which were small enough to fit in our pockets. Running out of the store we separated, each to go to our own homes. Naively, I showed Mother what I'd got. The price of each would be sixpence or a shilling I guess, much more than any pocket money I would have had available.

"And where did you come by these, Billy?" Mother quizzed.

"From Woolworths," I replied.

"And how did you pay for them?"

"I didn't. I waited until the shop lady wasn't looking, then took them and put them in my pocket," I replied innocently, believing this was no worse than pinching a few apples or plums from a neighbour's tree when they weren't looking, or picking blackberries from a hedgerow.

Mother took no time in teaching me the error of my ways. She marched me back down to the shop and explained to the manager what had happened. I was severely told off and threatened with the police and probably prison if I was ever caught again. I wasn't ever caught again!

Another incident of life-changing delinquency, which many an errant juvenile was guilty of, was when I stole a packet of cigarettes from home. Mother was a smoker and everything at home was a shared consumable - wasn't it? Although, I don't think I would have asked then, at the age of seven or eight, if I could have a packet of cigarettes, even though attitudes towards smoking in pre-modern times were very different. It was an adult allowable vice, like liquor, beer or kissing girls and not for children.

So, off Malcolm and I went with the spoils to the street air raid shelter. This was a shared defence, available for those who didn't have an Anderson Shelter in their garden. At this time, towards the end of the war, they weren't used for defence any more, the Luftwaffe having been largely neutralised since the Americans entered the fray. The street shelters had become dens for kids to hide away from the adult world for an hour or two out of the rain. In the nineteen forties more than half of the adult population smoked. During a bombing raid, when the street shelter would have been full of thirty or forty folks, with half of them chuffing away, there'd have been a fair billowing of smoke emanating out of the shelter entrance. I bet it looked similar on that day when Malcolm and I smoked the entire packet, one after the other. We were both violently sick and I put it down as one of the daftest things I have ever done. I'm not sure if Malcolm persevered with the daft activity but I certainly have never smoked another cigarette in all of my life. However, I did find cigars to be a soothing luxury in later years, toasting success with a particularly excellent meal followed by a fine brandy and a Havana…

Sometimes, on my way home from school, I would stand outside the gates of Stoneygate College. Jacqueline, my sister, continued her education there and I'd wait to walk home with her. I think it was a bit of bravado on my part, hoping Miss Knight would spot me and I could swagger in a 'can't catch me now' sort of way. Jaqueline was not amused which also added to my pleasure. She'd say, "I don't want to be picked up by a crook!"

Clothes rationing definitely had its upside too. I could only have two pairs of school trousers and it was mandatory always to wear school uniform. On a rainy washday, walking to school I'd find a nice muddy puddle, sit in it and then return home. Amazing! I couldn't then go to school because I had no more trousers to wear until my other pair had been washed and dried. I had some blissful washdays at home with Mother and my Meccano set...

I hated school P.T. and games in the winter. All the school would trek up London Road, hand in hand (YUK!) passing ancient tree after ancient tree. The girth of each tree was plenty wide enough to hide little me and Malcolm if we were

45

the last in line - and usually we were. When the rest of the school had gone, we'd turn about and run all the way home. We never got caught and apparently we were never missed. I would tell Mother that games had been cancelled and she always seemed pleased to have me back home. She would feed me with buns, bread and delicious soup.

By my ninth birthday, I think Mother, Father and the Captains Rudd and Cook felt they had done all they could with my spirit. They concluded that whilst there were still two choices left for me, it was time to choose before there were none. It was either Borstal or Boarding School.

Sister Jacqueline had already joined The Christian Science Claremont School in Esher the previous September, paving the way for me to join the associated boys' preparatory school of Fan Court in Chertsey.

In January 1947, amid the worst winter of the twentieth century, I left Evington to become a full time boarder, with no prospect of seeing home again until Easter.

For that first term away I was desperately homesick, lonely and sad. But the staff, being well used settling kids in with their Christian ethics, holistic life, balanced teaching and guidance, were very caring and supportive. In the second term, I had come to understand a little more of the ways of the world and thus began four and a half of the happiest years of my entire life. Even in retrospect, whenever I find myself thinking about my days at Fan Court, I'm enveloped by a warm and happy glow.

To say they broke the mould when I was born is, as far as I can see, a misconception. I don't think there ever was a mould. But, from the age of five to the end of my schooldays in the summer of my eighteenth year, masters, teachers, elders, parents and prefects desperately tried to fit me into one. As I look back on my life and achievements, I think that together they mostly succeeded.

I am a left-hander and this did not suit anyone who was responsible for my education, development and upbringing. When I tried to help him, Father would become annoyed and frustrated with me as he attempted to show me how to handle tools and equipment. He'd show me how to do things as a right-handed person would and, holding the spanner the opposite way to which he'd demonstrated, I'd drop it. He'd grumble something along the lines of "butter-fingers" or worse and then ask my sister, who was always somewhere in the vicinity and which forever annoyed me. So I'd have to work it out for myself. Even God tried to change me! When I was ten I injured the little finger of my left hand. The bone came through the nail and I was in extreme pain as I am sure you can imagine. Believing that the power of prayer heals all things, Christian Science teaching forbids the intervention of medicine for all but the most serious and life threatening conditions. Either prayer isn't terribly effective when performed in the midst of agony (interspersed with the odd expletive as may have been the case) or even the good Lord wanted me to write with my right hand. The injury took weeks to mend and my left little finger is still crooked to this day. As soon as I was able, I used my left hand to write again, as even I couldn't read anything written with my right!

My first term at Fan Court was as close to hell on earth as I could have imagined up to that point in my life. I had never known anything like it and it seemed as if the whole world was a desperate place. We were in the middle of the worst blizzards and coldest temperatures that Great Britain had endured since Victorian times: white everywhere and cold as cold could be. Thousands of coal wagons on the railways were stranded for weeks giving rise to a critical shortage of fuel everywhere. Coal stocks at the mines were frozen solid and could not be moved. Temperatures dropped below zero degrees Fahrenheit for days on end, that's minus twenty degrees Centigrade in today's money and there was no respite anywhere. Every morning commenced with a cold shower which to me seemed nearly as bad as what had happened to the Jews in the concentration camps in Poland and Germany in the war. That gruesome winter lasted right up until Easter and was then followed by the worst floods ever known in living memory. I have felt amused ever since when I hear younger folk complain about the weather.

I did make one friend in that first term. I told Father about him when he came to fetch me home for Easter. His name was James Hamilton. James had been at Fan Court since 1945 and we looked out for each other. Mother and Father were also very supportive during the holidays and by the time term began again, hope seemed to have returned. I guess I must have grown up a bit.

Putting pen to paper in the writing of my life's story allows me to realise, to learn for the first time even, that the person we are at any given moment in life is as a result of the ordeals, trials and tribulations we have endured or enjoyed. What motivates us to make the choices and decisions that change our future is soundly based upon the experiences that have affected us. The winter of '47 must have had a profound influence on me. I wouldn't be at all surprised to find out, if I were to have some sub-conscious analysis, that when I was making my way in the work place and faced with a choice – Africa or Leicester for instance – that the little voice inside my head, speaking from the experience of a younger me other than my adult conscious mind, would have preferred Africa. "At least its warm there, Billy…"

But I also feel now, that to endure something like that dreadful winter dilutes the fear and it did make me more able to stand on my own two feet - to realise that if one is to survive and prosper in this world you just have to get on with it. And get on with it I did.

In that summer term I really did find myself and discover what I was capable of as I grew bigger and stronger. In athletics I was amazed at what I could achieve: I broke all the school records in the sprint events from the hundred yards to the half mile. I became captain of the rugby team and vice captain in cricket and soccer. We had a terrific new rugby coach at Fan Court School. His name was Eric Bole, and he had captained Cambridge University two years earlier. He showed me how leadership and teamwork go hand in hand, especially on the rugby field.

We had an away game at Great Ballard School. We were thrashed 69 to 3 and came back in disgrace. Our coach trained us intensively for the following fortnight, which was brilliant in itself, as it meant we were excused any academic lessons. I led out the team for the return match at our own ground. It was by far the hardest match any of us had ever played. With two minutes to go we were losing 10 – 11. I knew I'd played well and couldn't have given any more: I had scored all ten points. We were awarded a penalty about half way down the pitch ten yards in from the touch line. Not the easiest position from which to kick for goal. No teamwork in the world could help me now I thought, it's all down to me, and I can do it! There was a deathly silence all around; the Headmaster, being a rugby fanatic, had allowed the whole school to watch the game. The whistle blew, it was now or never…

The ball rose majestically, almost in slow motion and sailed perfectly betwixt the two posts, as if guided by unseen forces it seemed. There was no more time. The final whistle blew - we had beaten them 13 points to 11. Revenge never tastes as sweet as it does on your home ground. I was the school hero. The Headmaster declared a school holiday and all of Fan Court went to Chessington Zoo. My life at Fan Court became much, much better after that day.

My best friend James Hamilton and I were not only heroes of the rugby field we were also champions of the boxing ring. But I do feel the odds were very much in our favour: we had both grown faster than our peers, James more so than I as he was getting on for six feet tall at the age of eleven while I was five feet eight and a half inches. I remember that my appetite was legendary. I could eat a whole loaf of bread with one meal. "Well you don't grow unless you get fed!" I'd proclaim. At one stage I had the nickname "Fatty Ford" but that wouldn't have been in the rugger season and I don't recall anyone daring to say it to my face.

James and I also took up a keen interest in model engineering, particularly model planes. We'd make them out of balsa wood and paper to the proper plans which were supplied. Aircraft dope is a plasticised lacquer and is applied to the paper covered aircraft. This tightens and stiffens the paper stretched over the balsa wood frame, which renders it smooth, airtight and fit for flight. We built some really fine aeroplanes. We got hold of a 1cc Mills diesel engine that wouldn't run at first. I stripped it down and put it back together a few times, eventually to a point where I knew it should fire up. We mounted it on a bit of wood and clamped the wood in a vice. First James would flick the propeller and then me. Still it refused to start. It was getting late in the evening and we should have finished, but we had lost track of time.

At this juncture, it is important to let you know that these little engines were fiery, noisy brutes. In the open air, at a comfortable distance they sound like a very angry, very large wasp. But in a confined space - and this confined space, which was the model engineering room, was below our teacher's living quarters - they sound like a Gatling gun firing off blanks inside a dustbin. The other vital feature of this awkward beast was that it contained enough fuel to power it for one minute exactly and there was no off switch. Of course there were no radio controls in those days, so when you had completed a model and were ready to fly you could fire it up and it would ascend to about fifty feet, go for a minute and then glide gently back to earth. We'd chase after it and pick it up when and where it landed. Brilliant fun! And we had the sixty three glorious acres of Fan Court grounds in the heart of the Surrey countryside to chase about in.

Our teacher was a very decent fellow, but he did have a bit of a temper if any of us boys tested him too much. On that evening he was on his way to turf us out back to our dormitories when James gave the propeller one last flick.

BANG! SPLUTTER! BANG! BANG! BANG! Off it sounded in a cloud of castor oil and ether smoke just as our teacher walked in. He looked as if he had been shot. Of course, no matter how much he shouted after that it wouldn't stop for at least sixty seconds and, let me tell you, a minute under such conditions is a very long time. No matter how much we tried to explain afterwards, the master never believed that we hadn't done it on purpose. We were banned from the model room for a month and put on special duties.

Friendships that are formed in childhood often last a lifetime, even though your lives diverge and you go your separate ways. James left Fan Court two terms earlier than I did, to go to Eton. He was born into what society calls The Ruling Class who usually go to Eton or Harrow and then on to Oxbridge. He inherited his family title and wealth in due course to become Lord Hamilton, the 4th Baron Hamilton of Dalzell. We lost touch, as often happens in life, although our friendship was re-kindled in later years. He too followed in the teachings of Christian Science, but prayer couldn't beat the cancer that took his life in 2006. I was sad when he left Fan Court and of course very sad when he died; he was a lovely person, a leader, a fine sportsman and a great friend.

My own time at Fan Court also had to come to an end. As a sportsman I could have got into any school in the land, but if I were to make something of myself in the big wide world I would need rather more in the way of an education. And sporting scholarships were extremely rare back in those days. Eton and Harrow were not for me – not only were the fees astronomical, you needed to have your name down at birth. Two schools were chosen for me as being suitable and possible: Oundle and Stowe. I was coached in Latin and Maths during the last few weeks coming up to the entrance exam. There were three factors that determined the course of the next four years of my life: I failed the maths exam for Oundle school and I got 58% in the entrance exam for Stowe, placing me ninety-eighth out of the hundred boys that were to be the intake for the autumn term of 1951. The third, and probably most decisive, was that my head teacher had written a glowing reference to the housemaster of Stowe explaining my strengths and leadership qualities and that in his eyes I would make something of myself in the right school with the right guidance. My housemaster at Fan Court told me of the letter during my leaving interview.

Father had promised me a brand new Triumph Twin for my sixteenth birthday as a reward for my success, but I suppose he hadn't reckoned on how much the school fees for both my sister and I would add up to over the next few years, because I ended up with a second hand BSA C11 – but I was never one to bite the hand that feeds…

★   ★   ★

"That boy will end up swinging on the end of a rope!"

"I will make sure he never gets into another school in Leicestershire!"

I stand firm and I stand first.

Motto of Stowe School

Chapter 4

Persto et Praesto:

As positively transforming as Fan Court School had been for me, life at Stowe began in stark contrast. I left the family atmosphere of a small, country preparatory school feeling like I was number one of seventy and joined the stately uncaring isolation of Stowe feeling like I was number six hundred out of six hundred. Despite the glowing reference from my headmaster I found myself immediately in contention with my new house master. I was at odds with him throughout my time at Stowe and felt then, as I do now, that I did not fit in the way he thought I should. I was a Christian Scientist and although I have never been evangelical about it, I made no secret of it either. He was prejudiced about anything that didn't conform with his view of the world. His name, to us, was Fritz Clifford and he was house master of Grafton House. He praised, encouraged and congratulated most of the rest of the boys in his house, all except me. This has had the most profound lifelong effect upon me. The pendulum swings goes the metaphor, and this is certainly true with me. I have always conducted my relationships, both personal and in the world of work, fairly and without prejudice, no matter who I maybe with or where they might have come from. When I think about it, and to adapt a line from that superb poem by Rudyard Kipling: I have preferred to walk on the side of those with the common touch rather than walk with kings.

My talent and strength got me through most of that first year at public school although my peers were now catching up with me and I was finding it tougher to stay ahead. Of course, there was also ten times the number of boys competing for the same honours. I gained a place in the under-14s rugby team and soon became captain. But my physical growth had ceased. I'd reached the height of five feet eight and a half, the same as I am now and my hormones had surfaced and started to mess around with my emotions. For the last term of my second year from May through to September I descended into a deep clinical depression. I really thought I was dying and was terrified; the aggression and bullying from Fritz was most likely the dominant force that caused my condition, but my house mates were very supportive.

At Stowe there wasn't the extreme fagging system that was prevalent in most public schools, it was a much diluted regime. New boys were assigned to older boys and the younger ones were expected to do menial tasks that needed doing around the prefects' studies: cleaning, polishing boots and belt buckles for inspections, fetching and carrying and so on. I know there was some maltreatment and abuse of the system, but it was certainly not widespread and definitely not encouraged.

In May of 1953, just as our new Queen was crowned, Everest had been conquered and rationing came to an end, I was sent home from school, medically depressed. My condition was so far gone it was felt nothing more could be done with me as I'd refused any medical help, therapy or medicine, due to my beliefs. The fear of the doctor far outweighed any other debilitation I was experiencing and so I was ordered home to rest and recuperate.

Father picked me up in the Bentley and drove out of the school gates onto the narrow road towards Silverstone. He didn't mention my depression and a couple of miles up the road he pulled in to a driveway of a large country house, and said, "Come on lad, move over, your turn now." The darkness in me lightened as he got out of the car and came round to the passenger side.

That wasn't the first time I had driven on proper roads, Father would often let me drive on the way home. I had been driving cars off road since I was eleven. My first experience was in a 1937 Hudson Terraplane - a big American limousine into which Father had fitted a four cylinder Perkins diesel engine, like the ones I'd helped Bert with in my infant days. It was on one of our holidays to Scotland when we'd stayed with an uncle on my Mother's side. After the war many of the old aerodromes used by the RAF had become abandoned and were excellent places for learning to drive at any age. A relative half-owned the land this one was on, it was called East Fortune and was about twenty miles south of Edinburgh, adjacent to the East Coast Main Line. The cruising speed of the Terraplane was the same as its top speed – sixty-five miles per hour. I could chase alongside the express trains out of Edinburgh Waverley; often it was the Elizabethan headed by a streamlined A4 Gresley Pacific or the Flying Scotsman on its way to Kings Cross. Of course we were no match for those majestic giants, we would run out of road and speed soon enough. I remember glancing over when we were side by side and seeing the passengers waving at us excitedly.

At the age of nine in 1947, it had been on that same aerodrome that I'd first ridden any motorised transport at all. During the school summer holidays, in order to deal with my adventurous ways, I'd be packed off to Eddie and Jean's at North Berwick. My second cousin had married a Polish man called Eddie Sanetra who had been stationed at East Fortune for the latter part of the war. When Poland had been invaded by the Germans in 1939, he'd managed to fly out and reach Scotland. At first he was arrested as a spy because his English was almost non-existent. But eventually his story was believed and he was seconded into the RAF to become the chief test pilot at East Fortune. He was like a second father to me in my junior years. He had a Triumph Bonneville 500 cc motor cycle. First he took me round the perimeter road with me riding pillion. Then we swapped around. It was like I had taken a drug. I remember the feeling, the sheer excitement of being in control of something so powerful, to this day. That addiction to power and speed is with me still. It is Eddie's fault I started on that slippery slope!

So, as a fifteen year old, although not legally allowed to drive on public roads, I was somewhat proficient in the art of driving. Father knew that if anything would cheer me up, it was getting behind the wheel. He usually let me drive part of the way home, taking the wheel himself again as we neared Leicester. Bear in mind that there was very little traffic on country roads in those days – it would be suicide today.

I remember passing Silverstone Race circuit which too had been an aerodrome for the RAF during the war. In 1950 and 1951 the British Grand Prix had been held there and I've often wondered if that's why Father had chosen Stowe for one of my preferred schools, it being only a few miles away. Father's other preferred choice of school for me, Oundle also was close to a very popular place for racing cars too, come to think of it. Perhaps he wanted me to become a British Grand Prix champion to rival Farina, Gonzalez and Ascari who were the champions of the fifties? Years later, I was offered sponsorship to join the racing fraternity by the chief paddock marshal at Silverstone, George Cook. He happened to be our Grimsby Manager and was an ex-racing driver. One of his close friends was Des Scannell, who was then secretary of the British Racing Drivers Club. I turned it down, not through fear, but because I was an only son and felt that it was unfair on my family to take such a risk, bearing in mind that eight out of ten racing drivers in those days were killed on the track. I don't regret that decision.

Memory fails me as I attempt to recall negative episodes in my life, perhaps it's a protective characteristic, blotting out my depression and allowing me to flourish again when it has passed. Although I can be sure that neither Mother nor Father would have made too much fuss.

Father and I set off in September 1953 to return to Stowe for the new school year and we hadn't driven far, only a dozen miles or so, when I told him I couldn't go back. He was quite pragmatic and not at all annoyed as I had feared he might be. He just turned the car around and headed back home. When we arrived and had unpacked my bags he said to me, "You have a fortnight to sort yourself out or you're going to see a doctor!"

At that age I was scared out of my wits about seeing a doctor. This was worse than the curse of the hangman's noose Miss Knight had bestowed upon me - probably because of the time limit! I think this was the making of me and was certainly the defining moment between childhood and adulthood, the watershed where I face the demon of Fritz Clifford or die!

Back at Stowe, I felt my confidence return. Fritz was no milder, but it was like I'd grown a thicker skin and he couldn't get through it with his barbed negativism; if anything, perhaps he saw that I had become stronger, more his equal?

The school motto, 'I stand firm and I stand first' pervaded all at Stowe and largely, apart from lessons, the boys ran the school. This is excellent grounding in leadership and teamwork, without intervention from any hierarchy. We boys had to work it out for ourselves. There was a military style training which we all took part in, with the older boys achieving NCO status as they were deemed fit. We'd have inspection parades on a weekly basis. I had chosen mechanics as part of my Combined Cadet Force (CCF) training which excused me from some of the more mundane stuff and gave me opportunities for driving and engineering practice. Also, I was able to exchange the traditional serge uniform and webbed gaiters for denims, which were much more comfortable. We were still supposed to wear boots, but a blind eye was turned whilst we were working. As ever, the rebel in me poked the blind eye a bit too often.

My Cadet Sergeant was Bill Shand-Kydd, a year my senior, who became a good friend as the months and years rolled by. He was a cousin to Mrs Shand-Kydd who was Diana Spencer's mother. On an early inspection of our group he challenged me as to why I was wearing shoes. I told him I had lost one of my boots. On the next inspection he challenged me again. I informed him that I had now lost the other one. Bill knew I was trying it on and appealed to my better nature, respectfully and with gentlemanly authority. On the next inspection I had the shiniest boots I ever wore. Bill was a great character, even if he had been born with the proverbial silver spoon to use at will. Norman Shand-Kydd, Bill's grandfather, had begun a wallpaper manufacturing business in 1891 which had grown to become a global brand, assuring considerable wealth for the family for generations to follow. After national service in the Grenadier Guards, Bill became a bit of a playboy by his own definition, pursuing a daredevil lifestyle. He was a successful National Hunt jockey, riding in the 1966 Grand National, and winning the National Hunt Chase at Cheltenham Festival in 1973. Thereafter he became a successful horse breeder, champion offshore power boat racer, property developer and philanthropic investor in start-up companies.

He was related by marriage not only to Princess Diana but also to Lord Lucan. I would guess that he knew exactly what happened to Lucan, but he would never betray a friend. At the time he professed strongly that Lord Lucan would never have done such a thing as to kill another human being, declaring that he was just not capable.

After a horse riding accident in 1995 he became paralysed from the neck down, but with his inimitable optimism he refused to succumb to self-pity and continued to pursue many of his interests with a touching vigour, inventing ingenious ways around his condition. He retained his engaging and flirtatious sense of humour and managed to maintain an atmosphere of jollity in the house which he and his wife Christina shared with an army of helpers.

"There's no such thing as privacy, but I keep my nurses laughing," Shand-Kydd told an interviewer, adding, "I've joked my way through my life and my memories are very sustaining."

After his accident Bill threw his formidable energies into raising hundreds of thousands of pounds for the charity Spinal Research, including taking part in a tandem 12,000ft skydive, complete with respirator, which raised almost £1 million.

"I've always liked new challenges and doing things I'm told are impossible. That's been my philosophy all my life," he said.

So I wasn't the first to coin that one!

My ability on the rugby field never left me and I eventually made the first team and won my school colours. Probably the best match I ever played in was when we beat Eton College in 1955 thirty nine points to three and I scored two of the tries. On the touchline that day was James Hamilton. We met after the game and shared a happy time recalling our days at Fan Court.

In 1955 I took my GCEs, passing in the critical subjects of maths and science and doing extremely well in history and English. I returned the following year, but I had always known that I was better with my hands than in any academic capacity. Machines don't bully you, they can be tamed and are, in the main, predictable.

As Bert had said to me when I was three years old, "You'll be an engine engineer, one day."

★   ★   ★

I remember the feeling, the sheer excitement of being in control of something so powerful, to this day. That addiction to power and speed is with me still. It is Eddie's fault I started on that slippery slope!

Accident...

Two roads diverged in a yellow wood, and I –
I took the one less travelled by,
and that has made all the difference.

From "The Road Not Taken"
by Robert Frost

Chapter 5

The Apprentice

When I muse upon what would have happened in my life had I not taken this step or that, I find it is the time leading up to my coming of age, the years between leaving Stowe and finishing my apprenticeship, which set my direction in life irrevocably. The steps taken then, mostly of my choosing but some seriously not, laid down the path which would define the course of my life...

Father would have liked me to go to university, to study law or something and become 'a professional' - whatever they were - or are! But university never held any sway for me, not as they were in the 50s. Being taken by Father to work at the garage from the earliest age of my memories must have planted a seed in me, I suppose, because I never wanted anything else. In September 1955, I began a City and Guilds course in mechanical engineering at Leicester Polytechnic, which is now De Montfort University. But every day was a waste of time for me; it was like Stowe without the sport.

Teenagers, then as now, are a species apart from their parents, and I was no exception. To be fair, Mother and Father had

had enough of me living under their roof at the age of five, never mind trying to come to terms with this post-pubescent heir to the Ford throne! It was made almost tolerable for them as we were now living in the relative spacious splendour of The Stone House, with its many rooms and different en-suite bedrooms around the galleried landing. This meant that we didn't have to be in direct contact all of the time we were in residence. It did have some splendid garage and shed facilities where Father and I could get lost in renovating some greasy, wheeled rarity as often as time and circumstance allowed, but I wanted to work for wages. Girls had now attained the status of goddess, rising to number one in my interests and in order to give due deference to any dalliance, I needed my own money and freedom.

Dealer management apprenticeships were hard to come by, as there were only a small number per manufacturer in any one intake year. The three best that were possible were BMC, Rolls Royce and Vauxhall. Father knew that with Vauxhall being owned by General Motors of the USA, the training there would be far better than anything British owned at that time. For sure, Britain led the world in technological and manufacturing innovation in the fifties, but when it came to earning money and success the Americans were far ahead of the rest of the world. We decided that I would be apprenticed to Vauxhall Bedford and I was duly signed onto their books. On Monday January 2nd 1956 I reported for work at the

Vauxhall factory in Luton, Bedfordshire with indentures for my apprenticeship at the handsome sum of four pounds and five shillings a week.

I'd found digs in the vicinity with a Mrs Shillingford for three pounds fifteen shillings. This included a good breakfast with a hot dinner in the evening and the factory provided lunch in its massive canteen. With the ten bob I had left I managed to plod my way through the long evenings to Friday, bored but not hungry. Mrs S did not have a car and she allowed me to park my 2-seater Singer Le Mans off the road in the drive-in garage which was built into the house underneath her bedroom. She was the epitome of style over substance and had a beautiful emerald green body, British racing green wings and bright red spoked wheels. The car that is, not my landlady! But even with twin SU carburettors it wouldn't pull the skin off a rice pudding. Fed by a fourteen gallon tank and not meticulously engineered, a stink of petrol always prevailed wherever the Singer rested for more than an hour or two, causing some contention between Mrs S and me, over the fumes filtering into her bedroom. It could just about out-accelerate a frightened tortoise on a good day with a nought to sixty time of about one minute ten seconds, and a top speed on a straight flat road of just over seventy. And, by God, with that suspension you knew you were motoring. But, of its day, it was a tad above average. An Austin A30, the small family car of choice, could only get to about sixty mph downhill, and didn't have any quoted nought to sixty time. My best mate had a Standard eight, with an unenviable nought to sixty time of one minute forty-five seconds, which allowed the opportunity to eat a sandwich whilst you were waiting. My Singer, with its nine hundred and seventy two cc engine, was quite fuel efficient. I could fill up at Father's garage on a Sunday and it would get me to Luton and back and to and from the factory all week on a tank full of fuel. With petrol at around two shillings per gallon and needing at least ten gallons per week this was a tremendous help; without it I would have had to find me a lift to and from Luton every week and I would have had to cadge a lift to work every day.

By the springtime, I had teamed up with a couple of the other apprentices and we had worked out a way of escaping the clutches and confines of our landladies to enjoy a bit of freedom. Mother had a twenty-two foot Berkeley Ambassador holiday caravan which hadn't been used for a few years and I did a deal with her to rent it to the three of us for a pound a week each.

Every week, to and from home in Leicester, I passed a farm called Mackintosh Farm. Being early one Monday on my way to work I stopped as a farmer was just pulling out of his gate in a Fordson tractor. I got out of my car and motioned to him that I would like a chat. Standing next to the tractor I told him that my father sold and repaired those very tractors up in

Leicestershire.

"Oh does he now?" When I heard his Scottish accent, which was similar to Mother's, I informed him that I had a Scottish connection on my mother's side and my grandfather had a farm near Perth called Ardargie Mains Farm.

"Then let me tell you the name of your grandfather," he declared, poking me kindly on the shoulder, "His name was Frank Kynoch!"

Well, I was never one to let a 'small world' opportunity pass by, so I told Farmer Mackintosh of my plight and wondered if he had a small corner of his farm where we could park a caravan for me and a couple of fellow apprentices to live in during the week. Being Scottish and a farmer he wouldn't have missed the potential advantage of having three keen motor apprentices on site to help with any mechanical breakdowns as and when, and neither was I not one to mention the possibility of collaboration. We settled on two shillings a week each for a convenient little nook in an excavated chalk pit which had a tap just a short walk away supplying fresh mains water.

I borrowed Father's series one Land Rover the following Sunday to tow the caravan to the farm. Compared to the Singer Le Mans it was like driving an articulated lorry. She pulled the 2 ton Berkeley with ease and we arrived safely at the farm near Harpenden.

My two fellow apprentices and I shared the duties. I cooked

the dinners – hardly Michelin star, but plenty of bread, meat, gravy and tins of veg. Mother often sent me back on a Sunday with a hamper of food. Robin Scott-Fyffe would fetch the water each day and Bob Smith made the beds and kept the place tidy. We were all sons of motor trade businessmen: Robin's father had a dealership in Dundee and Bob's family ran a dealership in Windermere in the Lake District. For each of us this was our first taste of independent freedom. We joshed and joked through our leisure time each Monday to Thursday, partaking of a pint or two of Flowers "Dragon's Blood" bitter most evenings on the way home from the factory. After our shift each Friday we made our respective ways homeward to Leicestershire, the Lake District and Scotland.

There were about forty apprentices on our programme. Our factory days consisted of getting up at seven thirty, having a rapid wash and brush-up and clocking in by eight at the factory, which was a ten minute drive away. The first two months had been spent on filing metal to within a thousandth of an inch. The next four months were spent on lathe work, culminating at Christmas in rebuilding a 1911 Vauxhall Prince Henry motor car. My remit was to machine new first and reverse gears. After the rebuild we spent four months on milling and two months learning welding, both acetylene and arc. Two months crankshaft grinding followed and we finished off this part of the programme with panel beating.

The Vauxhall apprenticeship was renowned as the best in the industry and I can vouch for that. I felt at the end of my first eighteen months as if I had learned more in that time than I had in all the other years of my life. One day of each week we attended Luton College to learn some theory. Considering maths had been my weakest subject in my earlier days, and a lot of the theory was measurement and calculation, I surprised myself in my own proficiency. Everything seemed to make much more sense when it was applied to something that was physically there. I really was in my element; I never knew learning could be so much fun. Amongst the apprentices everyone was equal even though some of the lads called me 'Posh Billy' because of my public school accent. There was another posh apprentice, although he was a lot further up the landed gentry tree than I was: his name was John Dyson, a second lieutenant in the army REME division who had finished his two years National Service and had now taken up his deferred apprenticeship. He was naturally self-assured as he had been at school at Epsom College before doing National Service, not in a bad way but in a military way, if you know what I mean - a bit like a sergeant major on the parade ground. He had a Railton Hudson Straight Eight Detroit-built drop-head limousine which was a real beast of a machine. It could start off in third gear and still out-accelerate anything we had ever seen.

Our lessons at college were often conducted in the third floor classrooms. One of our teachers caught the wrong end of an altercation from Lieutenant Dyson one warm spring day. Dyson was a couple of rows in from the back of the class where there were windows. He turned around to ask in his most military manner, "Meacham, open the window, and let a little fresh air in, there's a good chap."

Bob Meacham retorted, "Open it yourself!"

Dyson, not one used to being disobeyed, re-asserted, "Either open the facking window Meacham or I'll open it and facking throw you out of it head first!"

Teacher, not practiced in the art of dealing masterfully with Dyson types, erroneously challenged him, saying, "Would you care to come to the front of the class and repeat that, young Dyson?"

Young Dyson was over six feet tall and wore rimmed NHS glasses which gave him a certain air. He slowly and deliberately made his way to the front of the class to stand next to Teacher and, in his most stentorian voice, repeated verbatim straight into Teacher's right ear: "I said, either open the facking window Meacham..."

No one in the room heard the rest, except perhaps Teacher, as the classroom was in such an uproar. The window had opened itself in the meantime and Dyson was suspended from classes for two weeks.

After my departure from Mrs Shillingford's I also did a deal with Father. His dream of owning enough land to grow barley had begun to materialise when they moved from Knighton Church Road in 1953 having bought The Stone House, near Market Harborough. It had eleven and a half acres of gardens, a six and a half acre field on one side of the house and a twenty six acre field on the other. There was a ha-ha to the south, which would have been built to keep any livestock or deer away from the main house. It was an absolutely beautiful place, with a quarter of a mile driveway set between mature chestnut trees which created a splendid vista each spring, flowering alternately pink and white all the way up the drive. In between the trees and all around them, thousands upon thousands of daffodils flowered throughout March and into April. You could pick basket after basket and not see the slightest dint where they had come from. There were four suites of rooms upstairs in the house, each with their own bathroom and dressing room adjoining the bedroom. These were set around a square landing with oak floors and panelled walls looking over a polished oak balustrade down to the ground floor entrance hall. Downstairs there was a library, a drawing room, two sitting rooms, a large dining room and a farmhouse-style kitchen with pantries, stores and utility rooms. Every main room had an open fire. It was as stately as you could imagine and yet still be called a home.

Father had bought the house from the recently widowed Mrs Hubert Burton, the owner of the John Bull Rubber Company, whose headquarters were in Leicester. Large houses were going for a song after the war and Father paid £10,400 for it. It was eventually sold in 1967 for £61,000 to Tom Wheatcroft, the property developer and builder who brought motor racing back to Castle Donington in the early 1970s. He promised to preserve the house and gardens and just develop the two fields. He didn't! Within a couple of years, after builders and thieves had stripped the house of anything usable – Welsh slate roof tiles, lead flashings, oak panels and floorboards - he knocked it down and developed the lot. You can still see parts of The Stone House today in those original new-built properties. The land has been developed even more since then and the latest blots on that lovely landscape, of which there are now eighty or more, each command a price upwards of three quarters of a million pounds. Such is progress I suppose. I bitterly regret to this day what happened to The Stone House - not the land, because it is a wonderful area to live in - but the house and gardens and I feel very sad every time it comes to mind. Such a shame as the likes of it can never be built again.

By 1956 Father's idea of growing barley had yet to be realised because business wouldn't let him go to find the time to till the land. The deal I did with him was to plough, harrow and seed it during my weekends. It was very suitable for arable crops because it hadn't been touched for decades, even centuries perhaps, as ridges and furrows were still evident in the terrain. Father had acquired a grey Ferguson tractor and a two-furrow plough in preparation for living the dream. He paid me five shillings an hour and I worked a good eight hours on each day of the weekend almost doubling my apprenticeship wage. This gave me enough surplus income to afford a 3 year loan which I took out from United Dominions Trust and I traded the Singer in against an Austin Healey 100/4. Compared to anything else I had ever driven this was like the proverbial wet and slimy stuff off the shovel! It did nought to sixty in ten point nine seconds and it felt as if the G force distorted your face. She was beautiful and affirmed my addiction to fast moving four wheeled shiny metal. She held the road like she was glued to it, and to my mind was the finest example of the class ever built in Britain.

Along with this vastly improved acceleration came an amazing increase in interest in me from the opposite sex and I had my first love affair, nearly marrying the beautiful Rosemary after getting engaged just as I turned nineteen. When we are young and first taste the wonders of complete togetherness with another, it's difficult to resist the desperate urge to want to be together forever. That was what happened to Rosemary and me. We met at a dinner dance at the Bell Hotel in Leicester after I'd gone there with a group of friends one Saturday night. We arranged to meet the next Saturday and as I was getting ready to go out for our first date Father challenged me saying, "Where do you think you're going?"

I knew he'd disapprove strongly of me going to somewhere such as the Palais de Danse, which to his mind was a house of ill repute, so I told him, "I'm going to a dinner dance at the Bell Hotel in Leicester."

Father didn't believe me.

"But you went there last week didn't you?" he said, imagining I was up to no good and that I'd be lured away by loose females.

"I work five days a week in Luton and two days here for you so I'm allowed my bit of freedom on a Saturday night." I asserted.

Father let it go with, "Well, you just watch yourself out there; all sorts of disasters befall a young man on a Saturday night, especially one in his prime like you."

Rosemary was the daughter of a Leicester tobacconist and I loved her even though I didn't smoke. For a couple of years we enjoyed our weekend relationship and we did sleep together when we could escape from the confines of our respective guardians, but I guess we grew out of it.

Like much of what you leave behind in life, when you look back you realise it was never meant to be. Like the golden daffodils along the drive to The Stone House our love was never going to last, what with me in Luton and her in Leicester. Temptation, too, always seemed to be present whenever I went out in town.

"Nice car!" I'd catch them saying as they passed - a girl's equivalent of a wolf whistle I guess. And one or two did catch me, for I was no saint.

*   *   *

After the workshop learning, the apprenticeship programme took us on to the factory floor. Vauxhall would recoup some of the money from the cost of training by putting us on the production line for two years before we went back to our dealerships to do some real-life hands on stuff. We went from the utopia of learning in the first phase, to the drudgery of hell in the second. The mind numbing repetition of placing thousands of widgets one after the other for a press to clamp them, hour after hour, day after day, nearly drove me mad. One weekend, at the end of my tether, I consulted with Mother and Father about my situation. Father was very angry with me, suggesting I had no staying power and would end up doing National Service after all. I called his bluff and gave him an ultimatum: to transfer my apprenticeship or I would join the army.

And so, together, we arranged to have my indentures transferred to Oscrofts, the Nottingham Vauxhall-Bedford dealer and I commenced work there on Castle Boulevard under the shadow of Nottingham Castle. Oscrofts were the biggest Vauxhall dealer in the East Midlands and I started as a

3rd year apprentice mechanic in December 1957. Dennis Oscroft labelled me with "the gift of the gab" and said I would find my way into sales one day.

The gift of the gab worked wonders in other ways too – but then there was a girl called Lily, who was the stores manager's secretary. The first time I met her, my gift of the gab failed to manifest itself – I was speechless. I'd had to get some parts signed off and the manager was not at his desk, so Lily came forward to take the voucher request from me. She was about twenty years old, five feet tall and perfectly formed in every way. In the presence of such beauty, I guess my jaw must have dropped leaving my mouth open in astonishment.

"You're Bill Ford aren't you? I've heard about you."

I don't recall what my reply was but it wasn't long before we became lovers, my gift having returned, and we were not just restricted to weekends. I remember we went away for a weekend together to Derbyshire. We stayed in a bed and breakfast guest house. She read poetry to me, Robert Frost, I think, as well as Wordsworth's Daffodils and I know I fell in love with her. This was a different kind of affair to that with Rosemary, more urgent and all consuming; to me she was the human manifestation of the goddess Venus. On the morning we were due to leave she was keen to get up to be early for breakfast and was in the bathroom brushing her teeth before she had dressed, uninhibited as new lovers often are – was it Byron who penned that? The sun shining through the bathroom window created a glow all around her; she looked every inch the goddess of all a man desires, and I gazed entranced from the bed feeling I was the luckiest man alive. And we were late for breakfast after all…

With the benefit of a life well lived I now feel the word love is misplaced. I have rarely fallen in love but have often fallen in lust – much to my cost as you will see.

I had to part with my beloved Austin Healey 100/4, as Bob Smith, my fellow apprentice from Vauxhall, had taken it for a spin, literally, and after several months of trying to mend the damage I decided to chop it in for the Big Healey, the 100/6. Although this had an extra turn of speed and acceleration and a louder roar from the exhaust, I don't think it was any better as an example of how a two-seater sports car should be.

I'd alternate my daily route to work in Nottingham from Market Harborough: either going through Leicester and onto the A46 past Mr. Waite's farm and onto the A606 by Widmerpool, through Stanton on the Wolds and Tollerton up to West Bridgford, or through the country lanes via Melton Mowbray - but it was all a joy to drive in the Healey.

When I began to work at Oscrofts I started getting up at 5am. Father was always in the kitchen before me with the kettle on the Aga. He'd be reading the Christian Science Monitor or some such and often say, "Overslept again, have you?"

That trend of an early start on work days has stayed with me to this day. I would arrive early at Oscrofts and get a couple of hour's overtime in most days. There were always cars in for repair or maintenance and I could just clock in, pick up a job sheet and crack on. I'd usually arrive just after Archie the security man had opened up and was moving the cars onto the forecourt for the day's trading. I'd also be the last to leave in the evening and this, coupled with the hardest and smartest effort I could muster, had the effect of doubling my £35 per month, so that I could afford the extra payments on my latest car.

The roads at 5.30am were usually empty and I had them all to myself. I was always mindful though, of the dangers of not taking care, especially in winter and how excessive speed can kill in the blink of an eye. I had seen all too often in Father's workshops the aftermath of accidents, fatal or otherwise, with blood spattered windows and twisted, jagged metal. During the December of 1958, because there had been early mists and the roads were patchy with the first frosts of winter, I had been setting off a bit earlier and taking things a little slower. On the 20th December, a couple of weeks after my twenty-first birthday on the 4th, I approached the brow of the hill coming into Stanton on the Wolds, travelling at fifty miles per hour. I know this because I'd checked my speedo' as I passed the Keyworth turn but I recall nothing whatsoever about the accident that followed. I only remember waking up in hospital two days later.

At the inquest 6 months afterwards they said we'd collided at a combined speed of 125 miles per hour. The driver of the other car died instantly and his passenger, his fiancée, was very seriously injured. I don't know to this day whether or not she survived. The drivers of the two lorries which he was overtaking reported that when the cars collided there was a bright flash, therefore the fuel tanks must have ruptured after this as miraculously the twenty or so gallons of fuel that had spilled onto the road did not ignite. However, there were no collapsible steering columns in those days and the hub of the steering wheel hit me under the chin, fracturing my jaw and gouging a wide gash on the right-hand side of my face. The front of my Healey had been squashed right up to the bulk head, with the gearbox and overdrive units smashing through it up to the driver's seat, crushing and trapping my left ankle. Seat belts were a rarity in those days but I reckon if I'd been wearing one, given the speed of the impact, I would have had my head ripped clean off. The precise details of the aftermath are lost as I was unconscious for the next forty-eight hours. But if ever I needed to thank my guardian angel for anything it was for what happened during those precious few minutes immediately after the accident. No amount of Christian Science mind over matter could have helped me then. A passing St John's volunteer stopped and held the flesh together beneath my chin, slowing down the loss of blood and hence saving my life. I would have bled to death before the ambulance arrived. I had to be cut out of the car by the fire brigade and was then taken to Nottingham General Hospital. When I awoke two days later, the first thing I saw was the beautiful face of a young uniformed nurse with a plaster on her chin. They'd tried to twist my ankle through a hundred and eighty degrees, to set it back the right way round, and I had lashed out during the procedure. But this had failed and it was touch and go as to whether I would lose my foot. Luckily, a very dedicated and talented Indian surgeon mended me, although I did walk with a limp for a couple of years afterwards. I was allowed home in time for Christmas in spite of feeling very groggy. Father collected me in the Bentley. Christmas dinner for me consisted of bread soaked in Scotch broth, solid food being completely out of the question, as not only had I bitten through my tongue, but my jaw was all wired up. My bed had been moved onto the galleried landing outside Mother and Father's room because I couldn't move unaided for those first few days. Father tied a string to my bedpost so that when I pulled it, if I needed help, it would tug on his pillow and he would come to my aid. When I eventually saw my face in a mirror I was shocked. I looked a bit like Boris Karloff's Frankenstein as the bandages were taken off. I would have laughed if I could have done!

It wasn't until June 1959 that the inquest was held and I learned the official details of what had happened. They had had to wait that long because, making a painful and slow recovery, I was not fit enough until then to attend. The verdict was that the other driver's death was through 'misadventure' because he had been on the wrong side of the road.

I started back at Oscrofts in the sales department. Dennis Oscroft's hunch that I would be good at sales didn't run true when it came to cold canvassing. I was hopeless. It was the hardest work I'd ever had to do. It takes a massive amount of patience to withstand "no!" after "No!" after "NO!" time and time again, day after day. They never taught me any of that at Stowe. You can't persuade someone who doesn't want to listen to you, never mind talk to you. It was merely a numbers game - you were just looking for someone who was having a good day with money in his pocket. The sales bit, once they are interested, is easy - almost the easiest thing in the world. All you need to do is find out what they want, how much they have to spend and match the two. Perhaps selling them a bit more than they asked for and wrapping it up as a bargain. But cold canvassing for that golden opportunity was like digging for diamonds in a desert with no map or geological surveys, especially in the austere 1950s. There was no way you could climb the greasy pole easily, as senior salesmen would never let go of their customers and any enquiries went to their desks first. By the early 1970s the marvellous idea of 'marketing' was discovered, which provided the maps and surveys to make the job of the cold canvasser a whole lot easier, but back then it seemed likely that I'd be made redundant or, even worse, sacked at the end of my apprenticeship in November.

I'd been called up for a medical during that summer to assess if I was fit for National Service. I passed all the preliminary checks, even after I repeatedly told them that I had difficulty in walking due to the accident six months earlier. They kept saying they would get to that later. I've met a few of those officer assessor types throughout my life whose only rule of measurement is procedure - common sense has no place with them. Feet were at the bottom of the list and the last thing on their agenda. I spent a whole day having this test and that test, passing them all with flying colours - well, with a tick or a number anyway - then a shift of the pen-pusher's spectacles down his nose to read the next part of the assessment. Finally, at about four o'clock in the afternoon they got to my feet. "Goodness gracious me!" said the assessor, "How on earth did you get this far with those feet?"

I had triumphantly failed – Grade 4!

I asked Father what my prospects would be for a position at Ford and Slater. I'd always known that one day that was where I would be and so I was interviewed by Tom Slater who offered me a mechanic's job. I turned it down flat and walked out of the office. He considered, as did Father, that I should start at the bottom just as they had all done. To say that I was offended didn't cover a fraction of what I felt.

Upon my arriving back at The Stone House Father completely

lost his temper with me when he found out what I'd done. But I stood my ground. If I'd learned anything during all my years of conflict against those above me, Miss Knight, Captain Rudd, Fritz, et al, it was not to back down but to move forward with a plan.

I too lost my temper and shouted, "I'm worth far more than you've ever given me credit for and I'll show you. One day, not too far off, you'll beg me on bended knee to take a job with your company!"

Father stormed off to work, leaving me and Mother to clear some of the contentious air. Mother was as close to tears as I had ever seen her.

"We're going to lose you all together aren't we?"

It was more of a statement than a question.

I re-iterated what I had told Father: that it was pointless providing me with such an expensive education, which had taught me all about leadership, only to begin at the bottom again when I was at the very start of the best years of my life. It was stupid and a total waste. Father, Tom and Ken hadn't had an education and had had no choice but to start at the bottom. Although Mother would never openly contest what Father had decided, this time I felt she disagreed with him. She gave me a hug, saying, "It's your life, your world and you'll get on in the way you want to."

A week later Father sat next to me at the dinner table, which was his way of saying sorry. His bark was much worse than his bite – he was basically a very kind and generous man, although of the type that couldn't say sorry in words. It seemed the argument was forgotten.

He said he'd been in touch that day with Claude Riley, an export manager at Leyland Motors in London, and an interview had been arranged for me the following week. Leyland were selling a hundred thousand trucks a year and were by far the biggest commercial vehicle company outside the USA. The prospects for a twenty-one year old were considerable.

After my interview in Berkeley Square, London I caught the train at Marylebone, arriving in Leicester about half past six in the evening. Father met me at Leicester Central station and enquired if I'd got the job.

"He asked me to go for an interview in Johannesburg," I replied.

Father, a little astonished at the location of the next step, asked, "Would that be as a parts or service manager?"

"Did you know he was their Overseas Sales Manager now?" I countered.

"I knew he was recently promoted."

"He said that I should definitely pursue a career in sales, especially with the experience I have in service, and I could go to the very top of the tree in the motor business."

"So you're not pursuing a service career then?" Father was getting angry again.

"No! In sales!"

We travelled the rest of the eight mile journey back to Market Harborough in silence.

★   ★   ★

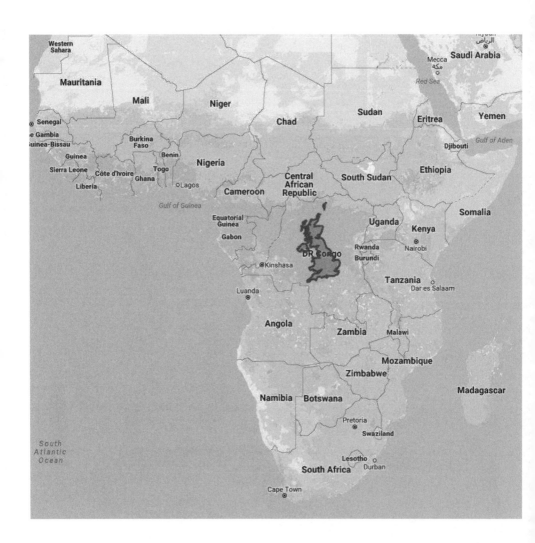

Africa in proportion to little old Great Britannia

Part Two

Africa 1960 – 1965

Cape Town at last

Twenty years from now you will be more disappointed by
the things you didn't do than by the ones you did do. So
throw off the bowlines. Sail away from the safe harbour.
Catch the trade winds in your sails.
Explore. Dream. Discover.

Mark Twain

Chapter 6

Sailing Away...

One week later, at the end of the last year of the 1950s, on December 20th 1959, I boarded the RMS Carnarvon Castle bound for Cape Town.

My father paid the £80 for the ticket and with Mother accompanying us, drove me down to Southampton in the Bentley. I have come to understand, from both sides of parenthood, how easy it is to be misunderstood. As a parent, with all the pitfalls and mistakes we make on our way through life, all we want to do is protect our offspring from harm. We want to help them using our own experience of knowing what works and, more to the point, what doesn't and we will state our case as forthrightly as we know how. But our children, beyond a certain stage of development, seem programmed to find out for themselves anyway, come what disaster may smack them in the face, or the backside, or wherever!

Father did emphasise to me on the drive down to Southampton that it wasn't too late to change my mind and that he could still find a position that would suit me back in Leicester. But at twenty-two years old, headstrong and with a bit of money in my pocket from the compensation I'd received from the accident, I was not for turning back. At that point it hadn't dawned on me that I'd never travelled away from the shores of the United Kingdom before, except perhaps on a rowing boat on holiday at North Berwick. My excitement for the new far outweighed any trepidation I might otherwise have had if I'd stopped and thought about what I was doing. Looking back now, I think I was possessed by a little devil that dwelled within me, pulling me on into the unknown. I mean, I didn't even have a job at this point. When I get to Cape Town, after a fourteen day voyage, I still have to find my way over another thousand miles to Johannesburg; then get through the toughest interview of my life with, as far as I knew, one of most formidable captains of the motor industry, Mr. Blackwood Murray, and then be offered a job. I was nothing if not intrepid, or mad, or both!

My relationship with Lily had blossomed, or so I thought, and I was totally convinced that I would get set up in South Africa and after a few weeks I'd come back to England to collect her. I'd take her back and we'd set up life in the sunshine and it would all be a bed of roses. All in spite of the fact that we'd parted without saying goodbye on our last night together, after a row we'd had about something and nothing.

The RMS Carnarvon Castle was an awesome sight when we got up close. The scene before us was just like one you'd see in the movies with a thousand and one things happening all around. Cars and trucks loading and unloading, cranes swinging cargo through the air on chains, people hugging and kissing each other farewell – women in tears and men with stiff upper lips, service men with kit bags, sailors in uniform. All manner of consumables, both edible and drinkable, were being loaded up the gang planks. There were men shouting from all directions at once and being in the thick of it was quite overwhelming. There was a band playing as I boarded – I've forgotten the tune, something from Sousa perhaps. Mother and Father came on board too as there was some time to go before the great Royal Mail Ship was due to sail.

There were garlands and ribbons, laughter and tears after they'd left the ship down the gang plank and turned to wave goodbye. There came a thick smell of engine fumes followed by a long, low blow on the ships horns. Then it suddenly hit me: this was as bad, if not worse, than when they first left me at Fan Court School on that desperately bleak mid winter day in January 1947. But this time there was no big sister to look after me.

The big ship eased her way out of port, along Southampton water into the Solent, turning east past Ryde on the Isle of Wight and then out into the open sea. I could feel the throbbing engines beneath my feet – two massive ten cylinder diesel turbines firing out 26,000 brake horse power between them, capable of pushing the 20,000 ton ship at speeds of up to 22 miles per hour. She had been built in 1926 and after her first refit in 1938 she had broken the speed record on her trip to Cape Town in July of that year.

It was still daylight as we left England but it was a grey and drizzly day, not the weather for staying on deck and moping, wondering what I had done. I settled in my cabin where, even though I thought I'd booked a superior berth, I found that I was sharing. My shipmate had been out elsewhere when I'd dropped my bags off but he'd already bagged the lower bunk. When I found out on his return that he was a man of the cloth, I was convinced that it was the Good Lord protecting me. I discovered that he was a devout missionary with a wife and four children in the cabin next door and we were to have some interesting conversations during our fourteen day voyage.

We hit bad weather about a day or so from port, in the Bay of Biscay. On a ship with no stabilisers I found out the hard way what real Rock and Roll was like. The Reverend told me that the best place to be when the ship was tossing like a cork was up on deck, "But make sure you hang on tight!"

The storm abated after a day but it left the ship more than a little worse for wear after throwing a bearing, rendering one of the engines out of action. The ship's captain said it had been the worst storm for more than twenty years and we were lucky it was only a bearing that had broken. We anchored in the bay of the Madeiran port of Funchal for repairs, having entered in glorious sunshine through water as smooth as glass.

My fears, it seemed, had been blown away with the storm and I took the opportunity of taking a trip in a motor boat to the shore as it was decided that we would, God willing, weigh anchor at midnight. It was four in the afternoon local time and with the temperature in the mid sixties it was just like a beautiful spring day back home – only the daffodils were missing. We threw threepenny bits and sixpences into the water from the boat and the water was so clear we could watch them twinkle all the way down to the bottom. Local lads who had swum out to meet us would dive in and swim all the way down to the sea bed to retrieve them. The colours of life there were absolutely amazing and everywhere around that beautiful sea town there was an abundance of all that a human being could wish for; this irony has stayed with me ever since – so often in poor countries life seems idyllic. Perhaps the people are poor because with a landscape and climate like that a person doesn't need much more to be happy. Perhaps that's what Jesus meant after all!

Ever since that first visit Madeira has been one of my favourite holiday destinations and I've spent many happy Christmases there at the Savoy Hotel, where the New Year's Eve fireworks remain one of the finest spectacles in the world. A dozen or more cruise liners always stop over on New Year's Eve to view them.

A couple of weeks before I'd been due to leave for South Africa, a girl called Dorothy, who worked in the directors' offices at Oscrofts, had told me that her sister lived in Johannesburg and that she was planning to join her on an extended holiday with a view to staying if she could find a job.

It was Dorothy who had helped me to arrange my tickets and we'd agreed to travel together. I wouldn't say she was in any way a "plain Jane" but on first sight she did not compare with Lily. Dorothy was taller, more like a business woman and she wore spectacles. She was well heeled, well spoken and older than me! I know this will sound unkind, but having had a lifetime to ponder, plus all the soul searching involved in writing my memoirs here, I do feel that the old adage, "Any port in a storm" may well be apt to describe my motivation towards Dorothy at that point in my life.

She and I had met up with a group of business types on the voyage and we'd all gone on shore together. We had dinner in a harbour café and enjoyed some of the finest vintage wine I have ever tasted - and it was less than two shillings a bottle! We watched the sun set as we ate the most perfect fish dinner you could imagine. I don't apologise for all these superlatives, coming from grey old England to this Technicolor dream world for the very first time, everything literally was superlative.

There were six of us altogether at the café and I sat next to Dorothy. On a different day she would not have been my type at all, but with a glass or two of that amazing vintage wine, a sub-tropical sunset, the sound of laughter, pleasant conversation and the clear waters lapping gently against the harbour wall, one could be forgiven for straying away from type and exploring a pasture new. And Dorothy did have a single cabin, better appointed than mine, although the bed was still a single one. We became better friends and talked a lot about not much at all, as one does with time and tide in one's favour. But, although we were friends, the passion I had known with Lily was just not there.

RMS Carnarvon Castle weighed anchor at midnight and at dawn I looked out of Dorothy's cabin window to see the snow capped Mount Teide on Tenerife glinting in the sparkling morning sun.

Two days later it was Christmas Day and we passed over the equator. There's an old Navy tradition called 'crossing the line' where those who have never crossed the equator before are immersed in water. In the Royal Navy it's a rite of passage for new sailors and is still done today, I believe, with much pomp and circumstance. It involves the captain assuming the status of King Neptune and his new subjects, called WOGS which means uninitiated, undergo a series of rituals to prove they are fit to serve. As they cross the line – the 180 degree meridian line – they are dunked into the ocean – and emerge as POLYWOGS – being now initiated.

Fortunately for me and about a hundred others, the Carnarvon Castle had a warm swimming pool on the aft deck into which we all had to jump at the firing of a starting pistol. Great fun was had by all and this was followed by a particularly pleasant Christmas lunch with the captain. The rest of that memorable Christmas Day was filled with merriment and partying. What a contrast from last year's Christmas when I could only consume soup through a straw! It certainly made me feel very lucky to be alive and respect each precious day knowing that life can turn on a silver sixpence!

We were racing south now at full speed and it was summer and sunshine every day. Accompanying us were dolphins and flying fish – a sight that truly took my breath away. As they leapt into the air through the bow waves cut by our great ship I am sure they were laughing at us and with us. It's a fantastic experience to be so close to such majestic, fun loving creatures - I believe there is an affinity between us and them. Not such a wild theory when you think about it for a moment or two, for we are all God's creatures after all…

I sent a telegram to Mother and Father from on board ship extolling the excitement of my voyage. Two miles out from Cape Town I received one from John Lamb Blackwood-Murray welcoming me to South Africa and advising me to spend New Year's Day in Cape Town to enjoy the festivities – "You're booked into The Grand, I believe, enjoy the food!" He said to travel up on the Blue Train to Johannesburg where we would meet on January 3rd and I'm sure this was my first test because he failed to mention, as did everyone else, that unless you had already booked a ticket on the Blue Train there was no way on earth you would get on it during the first week of January. On a map it doesn't look very far at all to Johannesburg, compared to the size of the great continent of Africa, a mere Sunday afternoon drive at most and in glorious sunshine, too. But it's a thousand miles, further than from Lands End to John O' Groats.

Dorothy and I would travel there together as friends - and that's all because I guess I wasn't her type either. As I disembarked I knew for sure that the only girl I wanted with me in my new life was Lily.

★   ★   ★

We hit bad weather about a day or so from port, in the Bay of Biscay.

The rhythm, the beat,

The love, the hate,

The cold, the heat,

The destiny, the fate...

AFRICA - Tracy Lee Eckstein

Chapter 7

Into Africa

It was a bustlingly busy place, the city that lies in the shadow of Table Mountain, especially on New Year's Day 1960. I was glad of Dorothy's company, but would have preferred the comfort of Lily to the pragmatism of Dorothy.

Staying at The Grand Hotel in Cape Town was really living it up in style. I felt a bit like one of the characters in the bestselling novel of the day, "Our Man in Havana" although I don't know whether I was the MI5 agent or the vacuum cleaner salesman. It was the best hotel in the city and the food was far above any I had experienced in my life thus far – even better than that in Madeira. But it's worth remembering that rationing, caused by the Second World War, had only ended six years earlier and Britain was still gripped by the heavy chains of austerity. We still felt pretty lucky if we could get an orange at any other time than Christmas. Here at the Grand we were treated to fruits I had never known before – mango, pineapple, melon as sweet as honey, red, white and green grapes, passion fruit and pomegranate. It was a real taste bud extravaganza. We enjoyed a pleasant evening, even though it must have been obvious to Dorothy that my heart lay elsewhere; perhaps I looked a little pensive but she didn't pester or pry, and I was grateful to her for that.

John Lamb Blackwood-Murray, whom I had yet to meet, was the son of the co-founder of The Albion Motor Company. In 1900 his father had teamed up with Norman Fulton and designed, developed and manufactured automobile engines and subsequently motor vehicles in Glasgow. The company became the largest engineering manufacturing business in that city employing one thousand eight hundred people by 1911. B-M Senior had been the managing director of the company until his death in 1929 and had also been the vice president of the Institution of Automobile Engineers for the last fifteen years of his life. His son had become a director and worked for the company until it was acquired by The Leyland Motor Company in 1951. He was to work for Leyland until his retirement during the 1960s. I was to be interviewed by him in his capacity as CEO of Leyland-Albion South Africa Ltd. He also had overall responsibility for the rest of the continent, the company being the largest supplier of automobiles on that continent at that time. Most of Africa was part of the Commonwealth then and order, stability and peace was the norm throughout the land, both politically and financially. It was a safe place then and a land of dazzling opportunities. Investment had flowed in by several means, some being spent on successful projects - most of those capitalising on the vast mineral wealth abundant in Africa.

One monumental failure of relevance to my story was the

Groundnut Scheme. There were many who benefitted from this folly, including me indirectly. After the project catastrophically failed, the amount of machines and infrastructure and willing and capable personnel that was written off and/or left in situ was mind boggling. The Groundnut Scheme was an initiative proposed and financed by the newly elected Clement Atlee's labour government in 1946 as Britain faced a severe shortage of cooking oils after the war. Peanuts were a perfect source of cooking oil and the project, led by Minister of Food John Strachey, eventually authorised £25 million to cultivate 150,000 acres of scrub land in six years. They began to recruit men for the "Groundnut Army" and 100,000 former soldiers volunteered. The first site selected for cultivation was in Kongwa in central Tanganyika, now Tanzania, where locals, it was thought, had already cultivated groundnuts. This may have been the case on a small scale, peanuts are an indigenous crop in many hot countries and in theory they do like to grow in sandy soil as is found in and around Kwonga. Strachey chose an old political colleague, Leslie Plummer, to be Chairman of the Overseas Food Corporation. (Jobs for the boys eh?). They had to build a railway to transport all the equipment from the Port of Dar Es Salaam on the east coast, a distance of more than two hundred miles. But the original target of 150,000 acres was gradually reduced to 50,000 acres and after two years, only 2000 tons of groundnuts had been harvested. The climate in

Tanganyika often suffers from long periods of drought, a detail that had not been factored in to Minister Strachey's plans. Later on in the project, the Groundnut Army tried to switch to growing sunflowers for sunflower oil, but a heavy, prolonged drought destroyed those crops too. In the death throes of that labour government the project was finally cancelled in January 1951. The total cost over the years had risen to £49 million (about a billion in today's money) and the land had been ruined in the process, leaving it an unusable dust bowl. Not the commonwealth's proudest intervention. But all that money had mostly stayed in the region and the Leyland Motor Company along with Unilever's United Africa Company (UAC) reaped rewards from the redundant spoils and enjoyed a fabulous colonial lifestyle both directly and indirectly.

A fortunate legacy of the post war commonwealth investment in trucks, machinery and infrastructure in South Africa meant that the roads were superb – much better than our roads back home – mainly because in Africa you are not hemmed in by lack of space. They were as straight as a die for as far as the eye could see and a lot further too. So, on January 2nd I rented a brand new Opel Rekord in order to drive Dorothy and myself the one thousand miles to Johannesburg. This was the German version of the Vauxhall Victor I knew so well from Oscrofts. It had a top speed of about 75mph and I drove flat out all the way. We did the journey without a rest in 22 hours, except of course for refuelling. We took grapes and peaches for our own fuel and a crate of bottled water.

I was to find that John Lamb Blackwood-Murray was a true Scottish gentleman. He was forthright, didn't suffer fools at all and was an easy man to respect. He picked me up at lunch time in his chauffeur driven Daimler Vanden-Plas from the Sun Hotel on Jeppe Street in up town Johannesburg and I really felt quite shy and reserved! However a person wouldn't up sticks a week before Christmas, get on a boat to travel six thousand miles across the world, plus another thousand in a rented car across unknown territory on nothing more than the promise of an interview, unless he had a good idea of what he wanted, was pretty stupid, or as JL probably thought, a good measure of both. He was off to Jan Smutts airport for a flight to somewhere important and he'd managed to fit my interview in en route.

We had a splendid lunch of grilled beef as tender as it could ever be, accompanied by some unfamiliar vegetables with a spicy sauce. There followed an introduction to one of the finest tastes I have ever known; it's still not that common here in the UK where it's known as papaya or pawpaw fruit. Its flesh is like that of an avocado but the sweetness is out of this world, so much so that Mr Blackwood-Murray advised me to moderate it a little with a squeeze of fresh lime juice.

As he put down his desert knife and fork, and wiped his lips on his napkin he offered me a job in the sales administration department there in Johannesburg, the biggest overseas branch of Leyland in the world, at the insulting wage of sixty-five pounds a month. I stood my ground and fought my corner, negotiating with every thought and thing I could muster for a whole fifteen minutes. He stood up and told me in no uncertain terms that I was untried, untested and unknown - adding that I would start on the following Monday and I would report to John Preiss at 8 am sharp!

"Thank you young man and good bye…"

I was taught from my days at Stowe that a good, strong, firm handshake, whether at a greeting or a farewell is the true sign of an upstanding and honourable gentleman, or a Freemason, but Blackwood-Murray's handshake would have dislocated the wrist of a lesser mortal than me.

I found a cheap but comfortable guest house seven or so miles south east of the offices in the district of Elandsfontein, bringing back memories of my time at Mrs Shiilingford's in Luton, but this time with a bit of money in my pocket. Dorothy also had an interview arranged for a post in Johannesburg. She'd told me her sister lived nearby and she was due to join her during the 2nd week of January. It turned out that her sister lived in a caravan on a site in Johannesburg and had set herself up as a modern day Gypsy Rose Lee. I successfully handed Dorothy over to her sister, thus ending our relationship!

It was hardly a baptism of fire during my first week of work in the Southern Hemisphere. I was given a desk in an office shared by five others. My line manager, John Priess, was a bilingual Afrikaner having been born and bred in Johannesburg. He was a fair man, good at his job and happy with the station he was at in his life. He introduced me to Willie van der Spek – salesman extraordinaire indeed! Willie was a fifty year old recovering alcoholic, whose better days were when temptation led him astray for an hour or two, but mostly he held firm. He was in his fourth marriage and as he said to me once, "My last, I reckon, coz I'll not live through another!"

As I have so often found in my business life, successful salesmen, those that bring in the results, usually see an angle on things that no one else has discovered. They get around the rules, even breaking them if they can get away with it and usually spend their commission on something frivolous well before the next payday. To Willie, every rule was just another challenge to overcome. He had cultivated a friendship with one of the supervising officers in the customs office on the border of South Africa and Southern Rhodesia three hundred or so miles north of Johannesburg. A hefty rate of duty was payable for any product imported into Rhodesia and this amounted to a good percentage of the sale price of every vehicle that crossed that border from South Africa. Willie would take a trip each month to bolster his friendship with the customs office and each month a convoy of duty free vehicles

111

made their way into Southern Rhodesia. Everyone in the office seemed to know about this, but the blind eyes turned and turned again back then.

Because of his ability to justify his rule breaking at every turn Willie had to report directly to Blackwood-Murray, as he was the only person that could tether him enough to specify the most necessary detail needed to fill in the paperwork appertaining to the multitude of orders that sailed through every month. Those tense meetings were attended by Blackwood-Murray, Mr B-M's secretary, John Priess and the very beautiful Cynthia. Willie was co-operative at these meetings for two reasons: number one, he knew he wouldn't get paid unless he helped them make sense of his extremely creative accounting which was prevalent with each transaction, and the second was that if he ever did take a chance on a fifth wife it could well be with Cynthia.

During my time in the Sales Admin office a new clocking in system was introduced to try and bring some order and discipline to the more wayward souls, so that there could be at least half a chance that one or two operatives would be where they were supposed to be when they were supposed to be. Managers and salesmen had been exempt from clocking in but this had increasingly infuriated all the other employees. In order to bring some peace into the South African Leyland world, clocking in was rolled out to everyone. Of course Willie van de Spek knew that this was nothing to do with him and carried on regardless. Charlie Moir, the service manager, reported him enough times for Blackwood Murray to get involved. The final meeting before Willie was made on pain of death to abide by the clocking in regime went something like this:

Blackwood-Murray - "Where were you this morning?"

Van der Spek - "I was at the railways office to get the discount return money on the last shipment to Salisbury."

Willie's monthly convoy to Rhodesia often went by rail and a discount would be paid retrospectively amounting to a worthwhile sum for the office each month.

Blackwood-Murray - "What time did you arrive?"

Van der Spek, -"9.30."

Blackwood-Murray, "And how long did that take you?"

Van der Spek -"Until 10.30 and then I had to…"

Blackwood-Murray - "I would have done that in twenty minutes!"

Van der Spek - "Yes sir, Mr. Blackwood-Murray would have done that in twenty minutes, but Mr Van der Spek takes an hour, and isn't that why I am here and you are there?"

Blackwood-Murray - "From now on you will clock in just like everyone else!"

Two days later Van der Spek was again summoned into Mr Blackwood-Murray's office. The beautiful Cynthia was not present. Charlie Moir and John Priess were.

Blackwood-Murray - "Why is it that after only half a day your clocking in card is full? It's supposed to last a whole week!"

Van der Spek - "Well, I arrived at nine o'clock and at ten past I had to go to see the tyre rep in the city. I arrived back at ten thirty. At ten forty I had to go to the toilet and I came back at ten forty five. At ten forty six I had to meet the man at the reception gate who was giving us an order for twenty ten-tonners. At ten forty eight I brought him into the showroom and at ten fifty two I had to go and buy him a packet of cigarettes. Then at ten fifty five he ran out of matches so I had to…"

Willie van der Spek was no longer required to clock in.

I had to complete a written test and a road test so that I could get a licence to drive the 24 ton Leyland Octopus - because you had to drive them to sell them. Willie drove me down to the test centre and told me to wait while he sorted out the paperwork in the office. Fifteen minutes later he returned with my licence.

"I'm supposed to take a road test aren't I?"

"You passed it, remember?" said Willie, "The Afrikaans chap who makes the forms out asked me if I could get him a job, I said I'll sort something out with the boss if you get this sorted for me. I just waved the application form in front of him."

"And will you?"

"Will I what?" Willie had fired up the truck and we were off down the road in a cloud of dust.

"Get him a job…" I was intrigued.

"Nah!" said Willie and that was that.

A couple of weeks after this Willie turned up in a brand new Borgward Isabella, a splendid example of early post war German engineering. He was in deep trouble potentially. He had used a company loan to buy the car, as salesmen and managers were allowed to do, but there was still a very negative attitude to anything German from the pro-British population. Most of the Dutch speaking Afrikaans were pro-German. This required another meeting with B-M with Cynthia taking notes.

Blackwood-Murray - "You know it is disciplinary matter to purchase a German automobile with company money, when there is a perfectly comparable British or American equivalent don't you?"

Van der Spek - "I do, Mr Blackwood-Murray."

I would guess that Willie at this point in the short proceedings, had the beginnings of a smug smile on his face, like a poker player who knows he has won just before he shows his hand.

Blackwood-Murray - "Look here, there are half a dozen comparable cars available and in stock locally. There's Fords, Austins, Triumphs…"

Van der Spek - "I would agree sir, but Borgward have just gone bust and they're selling all their local stock at twenty five percent off. There's nothing to touch this baby at that price and I know that Mr Blackwood-Murray appreciates a major saving!"

Willie was allowed to keep his new German car.

Borgward were a victim of the deep recession that hit Germany in the late 1950s and they couldn't survive the hike in interest rates that came with it. More than 200,000 Isabellas had been sold by the time the firm folded, which was impressive back then. A company called the Bayerische Motoren Werke AG filled the gap left by the Isabella with their newly introduced 1500cc model. And we all know how successful BMW became, don't we? The business world is littered with failures paving the way for others to exploit them and succeed. Often it's just a matter of timing and opportunity. Oh yes, and a hell of a lot of luck – good and bad...

Blackwood-Murray came into the sales admin office one day towards the middle of March and asked me how I was getting along. I was never one not to speak my mind and I blurted out, "I've never been so bored in all my life!"

"Really?" said Blackwood Murray.

The next day I was transferred to the Klerksdorp branch about a hundred and twenty miles south west of Johannesburg. The town was a main railway centre and a strategic staging post for all manner of commercial operations.

It was definitely a step up, but to my mind not one in the right direction. I was to be the parts and service manager running a team of two in the parts department with eight mechanics and two more administration people. There was a salesman, a branch manager and a girl in the sales office. My boss was Nobby Hawker the branch manager. I had bought myself a Renault Dauphine and re-built it over a weekend. It wasn't very pretty and certainly a good few rungs below what I was used to back in England, but it was functional, cheap to run and fairly reliable.

Nobby took me out and about around the area to familiarise me with the patch. He was an Englishman, bi-lingual and very pro-British. I said to him that I would like to trade my Renault in for a new Volkswagen Beetle.

"I'll sack you if you do!" and he banged the dashboard to emphasise his resolve. "It's bloody German, and I'm not having you buying bullets for them to shoot your own sons and brothers with!"

He pulled up on the road side, on the perimeter of a massive plantation of maize where we got out and I could view the terrain. The huge estate was run by an Afrikaner whose English was not very good and for the first half hour he and Nobby discussed sales in Afrikaans. Eventually I was introduced to the farmer and he apologised saying, "Welcome to South Africa, become a good South African, don't vote for the United party, vote Nationalist."

The Nationalist party at that time was running South Africa and had invented Apartheid. The man was very pro-German and had a pair of 10 x 50 Ziess binoculars with which he viewed the workers on the farm. He passed them to Nobby and then to me. From this view point we could see the ranch buildings together with the stabling and storage sheds. The white folks were armed and carried what looked like batons and horse whips, known locally as shamboks. I was shocked at what I saw. The white supervisors were treating the black workers worse than animals with gratuitous use of their shamboks and batons. It still turns my stomach to this day when I think about it. This was apartheid country, and the blacks were mostly treated as slaves or worse.

This is epitomised by a telling remark the estate owner made to me: "There will be no black arse sitting on any of the chairs in this house as long as I'm around."

The Afrikaans ruled here and if any one else from any other nationality crossed their path they would brush you aside, or walk right over you if you didn't move. Most of the Dutch speakers were very right wing, voting for the Nationalist party and had been German sympathisers during the war. But I never had any problems with the indigenous black African people. They were mostly polite, good natured, simple folk content to get on with life the best that they could. But the white Afrikaans were a very difficult lot to deal with.

I'd only been at Klerksdorp for about three months when

Blackwood–Murray rang to tell me that a vacancy had arisen in Tanganyika. I was to fly up in ten days time to meet with Ian Dall the managing director of Leyland-Albion East Africa controlling Uganda, Tanganyika and Kenya, reporting to Blackwood-Murray as his line manager. The job was to take over as the Leyland-Albion factory rep from the retiring Quentin More, based with our agents Gailey and Roberts – part of UAC. Here I was, at twenty-two years old, getting the chance of the job of a lifetime, or so I thought, and I was over the moon with excitement.

I did a deal with Nobby Hawker to take a few days leave. We had come to respect each other, my work ethic had no doubt shown through and I would imagine that Blackwood-Murray would have quizzed Nobby about my progress before offering me the chance of an interview.

I drove to Johannesburg and booked a connecting flight to London from there. I phoned Father and he arranged for Charlie Rowell to pick me up. Charlie was the parts manager for Ford and Slater who used to pick me up from Stowe.

I was coming back to get Lily, to set up my new life in Africa.

I had written to her and received a reply which suggested that all might be good for her to join me in this new life. I was so sure of myself now, having pioneered a new world and carved out a successful career path from nothing. We met for lunch at a little restaurant near to the Theatre Royal in Nottingham. How drab the food was back in England and how dull everywhere looked – no need for sunglasses in this dim place. Lily was aloof and cold in spirit. I had to prise the reason from her with an ultimatum – either she told me why she was being like that or I would leave her there and be gone. At that she started to cry. I have never been any good with the fairer sex when they succumb to that most impossible weapon of tears. She told me that she had never wanted to leave her home town anyway and that she had found someone else who wasn't so complicated with whom she was happy. Confrontation during tears is the precipice I cannot go beyond and I walked out, paying the bill on my way.

It was to be forty years before I saw her again.

I didn't stick around and I probably seemed pretty aloof myself to Mother and Father. I only stayed the one night, saying that I had to be back for the interview for the factory reps position. Goodness knows what my parents thought of it all, but they wished me well with a hug and a handshake respectively and off I flew.

★ ★ ★

"*I was taught from my days at Stowe that a good, strong, firm handshake, whether at a greeting or a farewell is the true sign of an upstanding and honourable gentleman, or a Freemason, but Blackwood-Murray's handshake would have dislocated the wrist of a lesser mortal than me.* "

Don't leave anything but your footprints

Don't take anything but your memory

Sign at Mana Pools National Park – Northern Zimbabwe

(Formerly Rhodesia)

Chapter 8

On Safari

Thoughts of Lily had dissolved with the miles between us and I was looking forward to getting on in my life. My interview with Ian Dall was the week after I returned from England and I had to fly up to Nairobi, the capital of Kenya, a distance of about 650 miles. Whatever preconceived notions I had about Africa were, at every new place I encountered, turned on their head. Apart from the apartheid regime Johannesburg was a good place to get on with folk as long as you stood your ground. Getting by on not a lot of money was easier over here and it was a more carefree way of life. Sure, it was hot and sticky most of the time, but I got used to that wearing shorts and short sleeved shirts. My old notion of how life might be in Kenya was drastically opposite to the reality. It was heaven on earth. The most beautiful place I have ever been, before or since. It is 100 miles south of the equator, which means it's summer every day with equal day and night all year round. It is five thousand feet above sea level which keeps the temperature down to a constant seventy five to eighty degrees; it has two rainy seasons, when it rains a lot, and a little rain for the rest of the year to make the flowers and fruits grow well all the time, so mostly you get blue skies every day. It also enjoys low humidity and light breezes. In April 1960 under colonial rule, it was well ordered and wealthy, if you knew the right people, and if you didn't the climate would keep you happy.

Ian Dall was my type of person. Younger than Blackwood-Murray so I could relate to him better and I guess I was his type of person too, for he offered me the job. I was to take over when Quentin More, the incumbent factory rep, retired in August.

Nobby Hawker was very pleased to learn that I was giving him three months notice, he had come to rely on me I think and this would give him time to find a decent replacement. We became friends and he would take an interest in my social life. I remember one week I had taken out five different girlfriends – we'd only chatted and smooched a bit for I was not one for sleeping around, goodness gracious me, no! Well not to that degree anyway, not then…

On the following Monday, Nobby was prying and wanted to know if I had slept with them all. I probably came across as a bit of a prude when I said, "Of course I didn't!"

At that Nobby thumped the desk as he raised his voice, "What on earth do you think girls are for man?"

Every time I took a girl out, he'd ask me the same question.

After I had made my futile attempt to bring Lily back into my life I was ready to make my own life in Africa and the three months remaining in Klerksdorp passed surprisingly quickly. I was treated with a lot more respect by everyone; there were a few bright sparks easy with their jibes – "It's alright for some!" and "Look at the blue-eyed boy then!" but it was always said in a good humoured way. I had learned a lot at Klerksdorp about the processes involved with importing goods and the make up of transacting commerce in Africa. The weather had cooled down a bit as this was their autumn and winter and it did occur to me that the best you get in England is about the worst you get there.

So I packed my bags, said my farewells and set off for the next stage in my African adventure, boarding a DC7C Piston plane bound for Nairobi. After picking up my company car in Nairobi and spending three days being introduced to the processes and people I would be dealing with in my new role as Factory Representative- Leyland - Albion East Africa Limited, I set off to meet Quentin More. His office was in Dar Es Salaam about 650 miles to the south east, on the shores of the Indian Ocean. My company car was a step in the right direction as far as make and model were concerned, but not in mileage terms. Ian Dall had taken the opportunity to upgrade his two-year old, light green Ford Zephyr Mark II for a new Citroën D19. The Ford Zephyr was then the largest UK Ford ever built and it really was a big beast of a machine. It had a 2.6 litre straight six cylinder engine and could achieve over

125

eighty miles an hour on a straight tarmac road, albeit at 18 – 20 mpg and only a ten gallon tank. My 'new' car, registration number KFU 221, had done 80,000 miles on all types of African roads – dirt track safari roads, tarmac highways, hot city back roads and mountain passes to name but a few. Handling them all with equal aplomb, it was definitely the right car for the job and was good for another few thousand miles for sure. In those days there were very few miles of tarmac in East Africa, with a few exceptions.

I'd booked in at a hotel in Moshi, which was about half way to Dar Es Salaam, at the foot of Mount Kilimanjaro. The highest mountain in Africa comes upon you very slowly no matter which way you approach it. Coming from the north I first viewed the peak about three hours away from Moshi - just a glint of its snowy top which at first I thought was a wisp of cloud. I realised what it was when it didn't move and it was surprising how amazed I felt even though many of my new colleagues had told me of its majesty.

Kilimanjaro sits on the Masai Steppe, straddling the border of Kenya and Tanganyika, which is three thousand feet above sea level; the mountain rises to 19,540 ft at its highest point. Because it is a single mountain and not part of a range, like the Himalayas for instance, it is probably the most spectacular mountain in the world as viewed from its base in any direction. It is comprised of three volcanic cones – Mawenzi and Shira which are extinct and Kibo which is dormant but still has gas-emitting fumaroles, although the last eruption was at least a hundred and fifty thousand years ago. Approaching from the north or the south, the base of the mountain is over twenty miles wide and from the east or the west it's about ten - about a hundred miles in circumference. At my first sighting I most likely drove with my mouth open in awe of such a mighty mountain.

By the time I arrived at my hotel in Moshi it was dusk and I couldn't believe how high the mountain appeared from that point. It was something I wasn't prepared for I suppose, coming from the very flat lands of Leicestershire where the highest point in any direction is Old John in Bradgate Park, standing at a paltry six hundred and ninety six feet.

I guess I was tired by that time as I don't remember what I did that evening or what I had to eat and I most likely went to bed early. But I vividly remember the next morning: waking at dawn and breathing in the fresh morning air from my balcony. The mountain seemed so close I felt I could reach out and touch it. As the sun rose I watched in wonder at its changing colours - through shades of brown to salmon pink and banana yellow, then to diamond white as the sun appeared over the horizon to my right. Even now, I can close my eyes and re-play that vision in my memory, like a film in the cinema...

After a welcome breakfast of bacon, toast, fruit and coffee I set off on the last half of my journey to Dar Es Salaam. Translated from the Arabic language it means the Haven or

Abode of Peace and in 1960 it was just such a place. It was the capital city, commercial centre and gateway from the ocean into Tanganyika. Even then it was still possible to imagine that a hundred years earlier it had been just a tiny fishing village. After the German East Africa Company set up its base there the area began to grow and by the start of the First World War a commercial centre had been established with more than twenty five thousand people residing there. To put it in context that's about as big as Loughborough in 2017. The Germans lost control in 1919 and the town found itself a British Protectorate, thriving in all its dealings. By August 1960 it had a population of about a quarter of a million, as big as Leicester is today.

The first thing I noticed when I arrived was how hot and humid it was and I wondered if I could ever get used to it. It was over a hundred degrees Fahrenheit and ninety percent humidity; just standing or sitting doing nothing at all made you sweat and the first advice I was given was to drink plenty of fluids. There was an upside to this – I could drink more beer and, for some strange metabolic reason, not get drunk. The New Africa Hotel was my first haven in this absolutely beautiful city. My room was furnished with a four poster bed draped with mosquito nets. There was a large ceiling fan for air conditioning and a fridge stocked with very welcome ice cold beer!

In Dar Es Salaam in 1960 was the main office of Gailey and

Roberts for East Africa, who were the largest importers of goods and machinery into Africa. The company had been founded in Nairobi in 1904 by two British settlers who had been surveyors for the Ugandan Railway company. They'd recognised a need for a supplier of hardware – nails, screws, buckets, spades, hammers, saws and all manner of building materials and equipment - to provide for the rapidly expanding population of prospectors and settlers in the area that would arrive as a result of the railway being built.

By the time I arrived in Africa the company was a subsidiary of The United Africa Company (UAC) and was Unilever's largest overseas operation. Every item that was imported (legally) into Africa had to be traded through an importer and in the East African provinces that company was Gailey and Roberts. They charged four per cent on everything that came in. Nice work if you can get it when you consider that virtually no hardware or machinery was manufactured in Africa back in those days. Most of the managers were ex-pats, i.e. cast offs from the failed Groundnut Scheme. Most of the workers were Asian Africans. The slang slogan for the wares they sold was "Everything from piss-pots to pangas" - a panga being an African machete. There were some derisory alternative names for the company as well but, with respect for our modern day political correctness, I feel it best to be careful how we air them here. Suffice it to say that Gailey was changed for a rude Swahili expletive for a disaster and Roberts to a common

Asian-African surname synonymous for those who might now run a corner shop in Blighty. Perhaps it is human nature that successful companies attract criticism in the form of unflattering alternative slang names, but they are mostly big enough, with enormous PR budgets, to shrug it all off as they continue to thrive.

Ian Dall had given me another name which at first I did not find at all flattering. I was known as Wee Willy and him being shorter than me by a good few inches made it seem even more derisory. In his broad Glaswegian accent the "Willy" was pronounced more like "Wulley!" But it would come to pass that he was probably the best manager I have ever had.

Initially it had been planned that for my first month as factory rep I was to shadow Quentin More. But that was foreshortened by the time I arrived and we were to go on safari (a trek to visit major customers in the regions) forthwith. Quentin was taking up a post back in the UK more in line with his background. He was a really senior diplomat and administrator, having forged a career in government service in the British Colonies and in previous years he'd been a colonel in India. Immediately before joining Leyland he had been General Manager for the Road Transport Division, based at Iringa, Tanganyika in the Southern Highlands in The East African Railways and Harbours Company, but had had to leave because he had been involved in a scandal. He'd had an affair with his housekeeper and had left his wife and four children back in England, bringing his mistress and her children with him to Africa. In those days, ironically, that was seen as pretty bad form in any government related position. Yet it would seem that today prime ministers and presidents get away with far worse misdemeanours. He was, though, in all his dealings, as far as I could ascertain, a true gentleman. True gentlemen, in my experience, don't make for very good salesmen and Quentin was a perfect example. He had only sold six trucks in the previous nine months, so it was inevitable that he would have to be moving on.

My first full day in Dar Es Salaam was spent loading up the car with provisions and paperwork for my first safari and buying some suitable attire for the trip – white shorts, short sleeved shirts, long white socks, sandals, and a decent sun hat. The two and a half litre Zephyr would do about twenty miles to the gallon, which could get us stranded in the middle of millions of wildebeest in the Serengeti, so we took extra fuel in two four and a half gallon jerry cans. We also took a couple of G-clamps in case of mis-haps with broken springs and an extra spare wheel - very good advice as it turned out! Essentials on every safari too were maps, compass, water and food, so it was just as well I had the relative luxury of the Zephyr to transport us plus all those provisions.

This was to be Quentin's last African adventure and he'd said he'd always wanted to drive straight through the Serengeti plains instead of taking the long way round. Accompanying us was his stepson Chris Greaves, who was fifteen. Chris showed me some family photographs including one of Claire his sister. To me she looked just like Claire Bloom, an actress in her prime in 1960. I know I fell in love with her at that very moment and that remarkable, inexplicable emotion has never left me to this day. She was photographed sitting on a rocky wall with a Scottish loch in the background and her hands were crossed over her knees. I whispered to myself, not realising Quentin was listening, "That's the girl I'm going to marry!"

We left the luxury of the New Africa Hotel at 6 o'clock in the morning and it was clear that Quentin knew the area very well; we called at a Duka, a derelict gold mine in the middle of the Serengeti, and were able to fill the main tank with petrol.

Over the years I have watched TV programmes about the Serengeti as well as safari trips and David Attenborough's are probably the best; but even they can't do justice to the real life experience. Wildlife is abundant everywhere. Upon first encounter you realise it is you who are the alien and this is their world. About half way in, after a hundred and twenty miles or so, we were driving though droves of gnus who hardly took any notice of us at all. We saw Thompson's gazelles leaping and bounding for no reason, except perhaps just for the fun of it. You can spot zebra when they move but not when they don't and all of this is played out in unrelenting sunshine with a constant daytime temperature of eighty-five degrees, mile after mile for hundreds of miles. The Serengeti is an area that covers twelve thousand square miles and almost all is untouched by human intervention. Only nature decides its course and has done so for millions of years. It has the largest diversity of animal life anywhere on earth and they all get along living there mainly because they all prefer to eat different things. Perhaps therein lies the secret to humankind's survival on earth – diversity. The Serengeti is also witness to one of the ten most spectacular natural phenomena on earth, the twice yearly migration of millions of different animals as they leave one part of the plain to seek food in another. We didn't witness this though, we saw them at peace in their season of plenty.

We left the Serengeti Plain and arrived at our half way hotel at eight in the evening. The Zephyr had mostly held its own throughout the day. We'd had a puncture during the afternoon, which made us anxious for the remainder of the journey with only one spare remaining. If we'd had other punctures right out there we would have been stranded until a spotter plane found us the next day. Before we set off Quentin had copied our route and given it to the hotel manager who let the authorities know where we were headed and our estimated time of arrival, so if we didn't make it they'd send a plane out for us. We'd also broken the main leaf in a rear spring and we'd sat at the roadside using the G-clamps to effect a perfect temporary repair. Whilst we were fixing it I had seen a light aircraft flying above us and I'd thought then that was a much better way to be travelling on this vast continent.

Our first destination for this safari was a town on the shores of Lake Victoria, Mwanza, where a number of Leyland Albion truck and bus operators had their main offices. We left the hotel at seven thirty the next morning to travel the final two hundred and twenty five miles from Tabora, now on better roads, arriving in Mwanza at the railway owned hotel at three in the afternoon, where we were able to change the cracked spring. A five course meal had been arranged for the evening so that we could meet the managing director of the Williamson Diamond mine, the largest diamond mine outside of South Africa. The mine had been founded by a Dr Williamson whose Indian lawyer and financial backer owned the only white Rolls Royce in the Lake Victoria region and the company had a fleet of more than a hundred Albion Chieftain trucks.

Dr Williamson's story is like that of a Hollywood film script. He was a Canadian geologist employed by a team of prospectors in the 1930s to study the land north east of Shinyanga, a neighbouring town to Mwanza, to discover its potential for diamond mining. The terrain was indicative that diamonds should be present and one or two had been found over the years since the First World War. The prospectors and Dr Williamson ran out of money and resources during the Second World War, but he found a new sponsor in an Asian

Indian doctor and together they persevered until 1950 when they hit the rich vein of gemstones that still produces more than three hundred thousand carats a year today. In 1960 it was producing more than three times that figure. They were very high quality diamonds too; one of them, the Williamson Pink Diamond was given to Princess Elizabeth and Prince Philip when they visited Africa at the time of King George's death in 1952. Dr Williamson had died in 1958, a very rich man at the relatively young age of fifty-one. The company was sold to De Beers and the Tanganyikan government in the year of his death for four million pounds, about a hundred million pounds in today's money.

During the meal that evening I knew I'd found my place in life – dealing with business men at any level and treating them as equals and having them treat me in the same way.

The following day we visited the Williamson Diamond Mine to see how they operated and to assess if we could provide a better service. I made notes about facts and figures, attitudes to the reliability of our trucks and so forth as we were shown around and I felt grateful for the time I'd had with Willie Van der Spek and all the advice he'd given me.

We had to be x-rayed on the way out of the mine. The locals had found many ingenious ways of taking diamonds out of the compound and no orifice was out of bounds for those highly efficient security officers.

The next day we visited the headquarters of the largest bus

operator in Tanganyika. They operated hundreds of vehicles throughout the country, one hundred and fifty of which were Albions. I made notes again, especially of their age, calculating what might be involved to start trading them out and, more importantly, when and I asked the question at the meeting as to the timing of replacements.

Mr. Prem Singh said, "We do not trade in, we run them 24/7 for 3 to 4 years then sell them on to Africans to run minor routes, which helps develop the locals' skills."

Quentin certainly made use of his old contacts from his Railway and Harbours days when it came to finding a decent place to stay. At each hotel, owned and operated by his old company, the manager was always pleased to see him, greeting him on first name terms.

Our next port of call was a town called Musoma, on the north eastern shore of Lake Victoria. The biggest operator of vehicles in this town was the Musoma Bus Company who had a mix of Mercedes and Albion vehicles. I quizzed the owner there about how he compared the Albions with the Merc's. He preferred the Albions but felt they were stuck with the Merc's for a few years, as they were newer than the others, yet didn't perform anything like as well. More notes went in my book.

At that time British automotive engineering was the best in the world: the Germans hadn't recovered from the war and the Japanese had yet to show their hand. Look at the world now, we're dominated by them and there's hardly any motor industry at all in Britain these days which is not owned by the likes of Mercedes, Toyota, Nissan or Peugeot. And yet we are accepted as the best in terms of workforce, engineering and productivity.

On day five we travelled further north along the side of Lake Victoria into Kenya at Kisumu where there were no border controls at all. Turning east we visited one of the largest tea plantations in the world at Kericho, which was owned by Brook Bond and run by English people. No Apartheid here and although you would never consider the indigenous Kenyan to be well off, the ones I met were happy, a bit cheeky and very likeable people. This was savannah terrain, with miles and miles of grass lands. It was called The White Highlands of Kenya, as settlers from Europe had colonised the area in the eighteenth and nineteenth centuries, attracted by the cooler climate and fertile soil. It was truly beautiful there: the climate was perfect with sunny days and a constant sixty five to seventy five degrees Fahrenheit. For me it was heaven on earth after the heat and humidity I had encountered elsewhere in Africa.

I did most of the driving as Quentin narrated story after story of what I was to expect from life on the road. Chris chirped up now and again and I had come to like him very much, but much of the time when I glanced back he'd dropped off to sleep. In Kenya, that was easy as the roads were now tarmac and the ride was smooth.

"When you re-visit on your own-some Bill, be prepared," said Quentin. "You've heard the famous line, 'Are you married or do you live in Kenya?' haven't you?"

I glanced back and Chris was asleep. Quentin continued, "Every Saturday night the farm owners and senior managers hold parties and at the end of the evening they all throw their car keys into the centre of the room; the wives pick a set of keys and the owner of them is who they spend the night with!" But I was not a man of this world... yet!

We stayed the night at another splendid hotel in Nakuru, called the Stags Head complete with gin, tonic and lots of bon homie. Quentin took us out to the shores of Lake Nakuru and showed me yet another sight that will live with me for life. It was then the largest flock of pink flamingos in the world. They were in a continuous line stretching as far left and right as my eyes could see; there were millions of them. The noise they made reminded me of the hubbub you hear whenever a flock of humans gather - in a pub, market or a school when they are unsupervised. All you can hear are syllables, shrieks, laughter and unceasing cacophonic chords. They say travel broadens the mind, don't they? Believe them.

On the last day of our safari we were heading to Nairobi via Naivasha, which was one of the original staging post towns local settlers would visit to buy provisions. Here was another lake and another cacophony of flamingos. This was almost at the most northerly point of the Rift Valley that runs roughly north to south for a thousand miles all the way through Tanganyika to Mozambique, cutting through the Masia Steppe and the Serengeti Plain. Chris and I followed Quentin who was surprisingly agile as we ascended the escarpment, passing a little Italian church half way up built by prisoners of war. At the top we paused a while and inhaled the view.

"Look out there Bill, MMBA!" Quentin exclaimed.

The view was sublime indeed. "MMBA?" I enquired.

"Bill, you are now seeing further than any other human being on planet Earth, with their feet on the ground."

You could see for at least a hundred and fifty miles, the air was so clear with not a cloud in the sky.

Quentin pointed southwards, "Just there, just out of sight below the horizon, is Kilimanjaro, just past the furthest ridge and that's two hundred miles. MMBA you ask? Miles and Miles of Bloody Africa! That's yours now Mr Ford, look after it won't you lad?"

We booked into our hotel, the world famous Equator Inn; it was the flagship hotel of The Railways and Harbours Group and boy, didn't they know Quentin well there. I have travelled all over the world since those days, but I have never stayed in a more beautiful hotel than the Equator Inn. The smell and the sight of the flowers in the late afternoon as I got out of the dusty Zephyr were almost overpowering. There were bougainvillea in full bloom, green, red and white; there were scents of lavender and herbs, basil and oregano I think, and hibiscus in rainbows of colour. All against the backdrop of a gleaming white stucco hotel. Our bags were taken from us to our rooms and we were urged to relax a while with a G & T on the terrace before we showered for dinner.

The next morning I met Claire and her mother Felicity, who had a flat near the Equator Inn. Quentin introduced me first to his step daughter Claire, who was even more stunning in the flesh, and then to Felicity, his wife.

"This is Bill Ford, Claire. He says that you're the girl he's going to marry!"

Claire blushed somewhat and so did I. Not the best start I had planned. She didn't speak to me at all over breakfast and she wouldn't allow any eye contact either. Afterwards, when we were on our way to the office later in the morning, I asked Quentin why he'd done that.

"Dear boy, I'm not going to make it that easy for you, now am I? Anyway, you've some wild oats to sow before anyone can make an honest man out of you. For God's sake you're still a boy! In shorts!"

And looking down at my bare legs he gave me a pinch.

I'd acquired an almost encyclopaedic knowledge of automotive technology, having been an insatiable learner of the subject since I was about two years old, and this allowed me to see the shortfall in the vehicles currently in service: that the combinations of engines and power trains (the mechanisms that take the power from the engine to the wheels) could be improved upon. The product that Quentin could offer was not really up to the job. The Albion Chieftain power train was the best in the business but the engine, a long stroke 4 cylinder using old technology from the Albion stable, was definitely not up to the mark for working in Africa. It worked fine at UK altitudes, but as soon as you got up onto the plains in Kenya, and beyond into Nanuki at twelve thousand feet, the engine could not get enough oxygen to operate anywhere near capacity and would lose power - or worse, stop altogether. I worked out that if we fitted all new vehicles with the Leyland EN350 engine, which was more powerful with a shorter stroke and a much more efficient air intake making it entirely suitable for all African terrains, all parties would benefit exponentially. It would turn a mediocre truck into the best in the world.

Armed with my notes and my nous I entered the meeting with Ian Dall full of confidence. Quentin had had his meeting with Ian before me and was leaving as I walked in.

"Over to you now, Bill," he said, with a hand shake and a broad smile as he passed me on his way out.

"So, Wee Wulley, what do you think you can do, then?" asked Ian Dall.

Glancing down at my notes, I looked him straight in the eye and said, "I'll sell you two hundred in the first year!"

We beat that figure within six months.

★   ★   ★

Leyland beats Mercedes

At that time British automotive engineering was the best in the world:

Let us once lose our oaths to find ourselves,

or else we lose ourselves to keep our oaths

William Shakespeare, Love's Labour's Lost

Chapter 9

Au Revoir Claire –
Hello Maivis!

Quentin and his family were booked on the RMS Windsor Castle, cruising to England from Mombasa the long way round via Cape Town. They were due to sail on the Saturday after we returned from our safari. I was so attracted to Claire I felt I had to follow them as far as I dare. Quentin had as good as given me the nod when I'd taken them to the airport in Nairobi on Friday. I calculated that I could get a flight to Tanga for a fiver, which was the first port of call for RMS Windsor Castle, meet the ship and get a ticket there to sail with them for a couple of days.

Being my own time manager now and deciding my own fate on a day to day basis gave me a freedom I'd never enjoyed before. So I could risk not being on call on Monday, get a plane back on Tuesday and no one at work would be any the wiser. Also my salary had tripled with my new job so money wasn't an issue anymore. My ability was now not in question, having proved myself since coming to Africa.

I watched the ship sail into Tanga Harbour, boarded and soon found Quentin and family lounging on the upper deck by the pool wearing sun hats and drinking cocktails. Claire looked stunning in a swim suit and I'm sure I glimpsed a smile on her face when she first saw me but then, with a 'catch me if you can' look, she turned away and continued reading her book. It must be part of the human biological courtship ritual, that hard-to-get stance that often seems present at the beginning of a relationship. You read about it in books and see it in films and plays where it only serves to strengthen the resolve of the male of the species. I've tried it since then the other way round and let me tell you, it doesn't work!

Well, Claire was doing her 'remote and aloof' pose on me alright and it was working – I was like a moth attracted to a flame. If I hadn't become good friends with Quentin, I could have been accused of stalking - if that's what it was called back then. By the second day though, she was acknowledging me sufficiently for me to consider that it was worth the chase and staying with them until we reached Biera. The only problem was I would need a visa if I disembarked there, it being under Portuguese control. We were due to be in Dar Es Salaam for a few hours on Sunday over lunch time having left the beautiful spice island of Zanzibar where we had stayed for twenty four hours. At that time the Sultan of Zanzibar was in full charge and Zanzibar had been a major centre for slave trading in bygone days. That would be my only opportunity to get a visa. But, of course, the Portuguese Embassy doesn't open on a

Sunday. The way of true love never runs smooth, does it?

But Quentin (obviously) knew the ambassador personally and agreed to champion my cause by accompanying me to the embassy. Sundays are very special days in foreign embassies; large, invitation only, festive lunches were the norm and this Sunday was no exception. We knocked on the ornately carved mahogany door with its oversized brass knocker and it was opened by a uniformed servant.

"It vill not be possible for zee Ambassador to grant your reqvest today, he is othervise engaged. I vish you good day, senors."

As the door began to close, Quentin stepped forward with a note which he pressed into the hand of the servant. In his colonial diplomat accent he spoke softly, very close to the man's ear, "It will be very much to your detriment and to that of your country's embassy, if you do not immediately give this note to Rodriguez del Qeza, your esteemed ambassador. Thank you!"

We were shown into a palatial marble reception hall and asked to wait. After a short time, Rodriguez appeared looking a bit miffed to say the least but Quentin, being a true senior diplomat, calmed him with a firm handshake and a half hug as if he was about to tell him the secret to winning the next war. He had advised me previously that I was to say I had a very dear relative who was close to death in Biera and if I didn't get there the next day it might mean that I was too late.

Obviously I didn't tell him I was going by boat as it was a four day cruise down to Biera, so I let him assume I was taking a flight from Dar Es Salaam.

We got back to the ship as they were about to pull up the gang plank. By running full pelt down to where the Windsor Castle was anchored we boarded only by the skin of our teeth. Claire and family thought we had missed the boat.

By the next day Claire and I had become friends and I felt that we both knew we would end up together one day, later if not sooner. We'd breakfasted together and dined at the captain's table. We'd told each other of our backgrounds, our childhood days and our plans for the future. I think our relationship would have blossomed there and then had we been without chaperones. We swam in the pool together, played table tennis and bowls up on deck and by day four I had won her over.

But I'd lost track of time, not realising how far south Biera was; on board ship, you feel you're hardly moving, just drifting along with the seagulls and dolphins feeling like part of the scheme of things and not getting anywhere in particular. However, we had travelled more than 1400 miles and after breakfast on my last morning on the boat I must have appeared anxious.

Quentin said to me, "Don't worry Bill, you'll not have been missed. All you have to do is get a taxi to the railway at the Rhodesian border then pick up a train to Salisbury; you can get a flight directly from there to Dar'. You'll be back in under twelve hours, trust me."

I never fathomed why Quentin hadn't sold very much in his nine months with Leyland – his knowledge of the world and how to get around was formidable. For me that was the hardest part of the job - getting from A to B, via C and back again. Perhaps Quentin had only ever been along for the ride? He acted as though he loved every minute of each journey though. I think his lack of business success was due to the fact that he'd spent his life travelling. Whilst in charge of the East African Railways Road and Bus Transport Fleet he'd continuously moved from branch to branch in a territory bigger than Europe, all on roads that had never seen tarmac.

Claire and I parted with a prolonged hug, promising to meet again when she returned to Nairobi from England in a couple of month's time. Little did either of us know what fate had in store just around the corner.

Going by train to Salisbury, I felt quite the reverse of the feeling I'd had when I'd left Lily behind in England. The further I travelled from Claire there was an ever tightening pull on my heart strings and with every clickety-click of the wheels the deeper the turmoil. "If only this" and "if only that" - endless questions and deepening dismay with every mile travelled. By the time I got to Salisbury airport I felt a complete wreck. Managing to get on the plane just as they were closing the gate, I wished I'd been blessed with Quentin's calm confidence when dealing with travelling matters. The thousand mile flight back to Dar Es Salaam took just four hours; it had taken four lazy days on board ship to do the trip southwards. There's no feeling of letting the world pass you by on a DC7!

I was due to attend the monthly cocktail party hosted by the management of Gailey and Roberts at seven o'clock that Thursday evening. I arrived at Dar airport with just enough time to get to my hotel, shower, change and get a taxi out to the ranch where the party was being held. These were pretty stuffy affairs with all the reps and managers strutting about and their wives holding polite small talk because that's what was expected of them. These parties were not even enlivened by the chuck-your-car-keys-in-the-middle procedure to look forward to at the end of the evening. I chatted to well spoken lady with a large bouffant hairdo (whom I definitely wouldn't have wanted to grab my car keys at the end of any evening) and she told me she had come out to Africa in the late forties with her husband on the Groundnut Scheme. Her husband had died in the fifties and she'd re-married one of the senior managers in charge of piss pots, or some such, at Gailey and Roberts.

I disliked cocktail parties and still do to this day and I spent the rest of the evening bored out of my mind. I don't think anyone would ever have classed me as the life and soul of that or any other party as my thoughts were all over the place.

But I found that work was my saviour and I focussed on arranging my first sales safari, working out a travel schedule that would speed things up a bit. The following week I drove to Nairobi for a meeting with Ian Dall as I would need his backing to get some of the transactions I had in mind through the system. He approved of my plan and I flew by DC3 Dakota back to Mwanza on East African Airways. Flying across the Great Rift Valley at approximately 7,000 feet and a speed of 160 knots guarantees a fairly bumpy ride. That journey though, was the start of the best and worst experiences of my life – probably ever...

We were met by the ground crew and escorted by bus from Mwanza Airport to the town centre, a distance of 7 miles. The lady taking us to the hotel was stunning and I found out later she was from the Seychelles and her name was Maivis. The East African Airways uniform, on the right body, is the most attractive I have ever seen: pure white knee length dress with a dark blue belt and matching hat. I've always been drawn to neatness and co-ordination – in many areas of my life.

I had time to change for dinner and on going down to the bar I was welcomed by Maivis who was having a drink with the captain, Paddy O'Reilly, and they invited me to join them at their table. Maivis sat next to me during the meal and I guess 'catch me if you can' is not part of the culture of someone born and bred in the Seychelles. That she only had eyes for me was only half of it and when we left the table to go for drinks in the lounge, she whispered in my ear, "You stay vith me tonight? I show you how vee come together, yes?"

You could have knocked me down with a feather...

Paddy had left as soon as he had finished his meal as he was flying early the next day and I shamefully admit that all thoughts of Claire vanished. Believe it or not, even with my experience with Rosemary, Lily and those few casual flings with the girls in Johannesburg I was still naive in the ways of women. I didn't have much of a notion of what Maivis was offering, but there was no way on earth I was going to turn the invitation down, Claire or no Claire. And, anyway, Quentin had said I had some wild oats to sow first.

Within two minutes of us entering my room, we were on the big four poster bed underneath the mozzie net both as naked as the day we were born.

Of course I'd had sex lessons at Stowe and it being a public school of some repute, those lessons were conducted by a Harley Street consultant, Dr. Livie-Noble (we boys pronounced it No-balls). Our lessons did not include anything to do with what the girl might experience, other than she would get pregnant if we weren't careful. I remember it did make the whole affair seem very clinical and a bit seedy if truth be known, especially in the lesson where he passed the condoms around. So, it will not surprise you now when I tell you that I hadn't ever thought a girl could also experience an orgasm. It wasn't long before this myth was blown away in the fastest learning curve of my life!

Afterwards, as she lay beneath me limp and unresponsive, I really thought I'd killed her - that she'd suffered a heart attack or a seizure. Then, after several very long seconds, she took in a deep breath opened her eyes and said, "See, vee come together very good!"

Some crazy days and wild nights followed that first 'coming together' with Maivis. Whenever I visited Mwanza, which was many times, and later when she had transferred to Nairobi, Maivis would be there and over the following weeks and months my education concerning the ways of women continued, all alongside my increasing sales success throughout my territory of East Africa. During those foot loose and fancy free days of the early 1960s I was merely doing what Quentin had advised and Maivis was just one of my girlfriends. Maybe I didn't have a girl in every port but there weren't many lonely nights I endured back then.

Just prior to Mother and Father visiting me for the first time in Africa, Maivis dropped a bombshell on me - she was pregnant. Our relationship had never been more than a casual affair - steamy and exciting for sure - but we hadn't ever professed undying love or promised to spend our lives exclusively together. Clearly though I should have listened to my Harley Street tutor a little more intently, especially during the condom lesson. This was also just before that great liberator, the Pill, had reached the lands of Africa.

She pleaded with me to marry her. I didn't know which way to turn. I was flying in my career and this was not part of my plans at all. Morally, for each of us, abortion was completely out of the question and it was also against the law. It sounds a bit callous now, I suppose, but I agreed that I would marry her if the baby were to be adopted as soon as it was born. I was surprised when she agreed straightaway. Through an agency we found a lovely childless couple who lived in Rhodesia and we visited them before the event. I also made Maivis agree to keep this quiet from our circle of friends and contacts and especially from my mother and father, whom Maivis was to meet for the first time when they visited in December.

Father was rather taken aback, to say the least, when he first met Maivis. Although she was extremely attractive, I don't believe he had ever considered that I might have a mixed race girlfriend. In fact he couldn't have been more put out if Maivis had been my boyfriend! He'd been born and bred in middle England and had hardly ever set foot on foreign soil or mixed with anyone other than white English people. In his eyes it just wasn't done and I think he felt glad I was far enough away from home to avoid any gossip reaching the ears of his workforce. My mother however, was her usual *c'est la vie* self and after a day or two she and Maivis were getting on splendidly.

I was able to take Mother and Father around with me on my travels and Maivis came too. By this time I had come to know my way around pretty well and was able to pick out the best places to take them. The first hotel we stayed at was the New Africa Hotel in Dar Es Salaam. When we met for dinner Father asked me what he should have to drink. Bear in mind that he was a fairly devout practicing Christian Scientist who, as part of his practice, would not drink alcohol.

I said, rather wickedly, "Oh, you'll be alright with the African lager."

"Is it alcoholic?" he asked.

"Oh no, not much at all really…"

African lager was served in litres and it was pretty strong, especially if you'd hardly ever touched a drop in your life before. After his second glass Father remarked, "Rather good this, er, what's-its-name - lager? Are you sure there's no alcohol in it?"

After a sumptuous five course meal and his third glass he declared, "I'm feeling particularly silly right now…" and took himself off to bed.

Father was to down a good few litres during the course of their two week stay in Africa and, I might add, he was always first at the bar each evening.

An old adage which I've found holds true is this: 'If you want something doing, ask a busy person' and I was able to escort

Mother and Father around while my work flow hardly changed. We even drove all the way down the Rift Valley into Rhodesia at the weekend to Victoria Falls, which was a fifteen hundred mile trip taking three days with hotel stops along the way.

Mother and Father would have stayed in the Falls area longer if they could but Maivis had to be back in Nairobi to resume work and I was due to report into Gailey and Roberts, so we headed northwards back to Dar' where Maivis could get a flight. Mother and Father had been planning to enjoy a few days there before taking a cruise to Cape Town but Father became quite ill with the heat. (Not the alcohol!) We dropped him off at a town called Mbeya which was much cooler, standing at six thousand feet above sea level. I booked him into a Railway and Harbours hotel and made sure he was attended to while the rest of us carried on to Dar'.

Returning to collect him five days later after he'd recovered, I realised poor old Father had been suffering from more than just the heat and this had been quite embarrassing for him. Commonly referred to as Dhobi Itch, it's a rash in the groin caused from sweating and walking about more than you are used to; it needs ointment and rest from normal movement in order to stop the constant aggravation and to get rid of it. He was fine again when I picked him up and I think he'd needed the rest anyway. I couldn't help wondering if he'd been down to the bar each evening for a pint or two of African lager!

In all we had travelled six thousand miles in two weeks, most of it by car. We'd mainly kept to good, well maintained roads and had taken a train the last couple of hundred miles to the Victoria Falls and back.

Mother and Father went off on the boat from Dar' to Cape Town intending to see a bit of Africa from the ocean before getting their flight back to London. I saw them only once over the next two years, as business almost completely took over my life.

Maivis spent the last few months of her pregnancy with her parents who lived in Nairobi at that time and we were married in 1963. Our time together after the bombshell wasn't nearly as exciting, as I'm sure you can guess. We got a house in Karen just under the Ngong hills about 10 miles from Nairobi and Maivis resumed her job with the airline there. We went through the motions of marriage to all intents and purposes, but after her mother and father went to live in Australia, Mavis would visit them often and each visit would be longer than the last. Meanwhile my business success knew no bounds…

★   ★   ★

The gull sees farthest who flies highest –

Richard Bach,

Jonathan Livingston Seagull

Chapter 10

Up, Up and Away...

I had driven more than seventy five thousand miles in one year on the roads in Africa. The Zephyr had given up with a broken crankshaft almost on the first anniversary of my arrival in Cape Town. Leyland having the Standard Triumph agency, I then opted for the Mk III Vanguard which on paper looked suitable, but after two months the bulkhead and front suspension had dropped by two and a half inches and the car had to be scrapped; it had never been built for the rough roads on safari. I then decided to buy my own car which I was allowed to do as long as it wasn't a German one. I chose a most unlikely make and model, but it turned out to be the most reliable and fit for purpose car I've ever had. I bought the 803cc Saab 96. Its two stroke engine required a mix of two pints of a special type of oil with every eight gallons of petrol. I travelled 128,000 miles in that amazing car and the only reason I changed it was because of my decision to come home. Our African Sales Manager Morrisson Wawaru bought it from me and ran it for several years afterwards.

In the summer of 1964 at the age of twenty six, after three and a half of the most momentous years of my life, I was promoted to Sales and Service Director of Leyland Motors East Africa. I had established Leyland as the market leader in that part of the world from a position of being hardly in the running when I began. Of course, I didn't do it all on my own, and neither did I do it by playing entirely by the rules.

Let me share a little of my wayward ways with you...

Leyland's East Africa HQ was in Nairobi where Ian Dall, the MD of this division, had his office. Donald Stokes was the Sales Director of the worldwide operations of Leyland and he was a no-nonsense businessman who happened to have married the daughter of Sir Henry Spurrier, one of the founders of the company. But don't let that fool you into thinking he was not worthy of the job; on the contrary, it was because of Donald Stokes, soon to be Sir Donald and by the end of his business career Lord Stokes, that Leyland became one of the five biggest automotive manufacturers in the world. I remain extremely proud of having worked for him and despite a lot of criticism he was extremely good to work for as long as you were prepared to work hard and produce results.

Company policy was that trade-ins were never allowed. We sold new vehicles and that was that. All trade-ins went back to Gailey and Roberts, ostensibly to sell through the motor trade. But they were so useless that they rarely got around to doing anything with the trade-ins which just accumulated as time went on. So much so, that when a Gailey and Roberts branch was subject to an audit they moved all the surplus trade-ins over to the next branch and then back again when the finance personnel had gone. To me, this seemed a huge waste of profit when we could easily sell them on ourselves and increase our own bottom line.

I was about six months into the job and we were selling more than ever before in our region; so much more that Donald Stokes came on an unscheduled visit to see what was going on. I had recently done a deal with the Matchakos Bus Company and traded out 36 Mercedes buses. With a good measure of Willie van der Spek-style creative accounting, I'd managed to increase the profitability of the deal by a thousand pounds per vehicle. I'd created new upgrade opportunities a year or so down the line and also increased the market because the old buses were sold on to local people who could open up new bus routes with them. Part of the deal was to give the old buses a bit of a spruce up in our workshops, which just happened to be at the time of Donald's visit.

Ian Dall asked me to show Donald around the compound – thus making me explain the presence of 36 Mercedes vehicles in a Leyland works facility. As the Merc' buses came into view standing in two neat semi-circles, gleaming in the sunshine, Donald Stokes' jaw dropped, "Who owns those?"

"You do, Mr Stokes,"

"HOW?" he yelled.

I told him the tale, ending by saying, "We'll make twenty thousand shillings on each bus when they're sold next month."

It seems hard to understand, but in those days a complete bus chassis was £5,000 and the body, which was hand made by African people working in an Asian owned workshop, was only a thousand pounds, making a total cost of £6,000. This meant that if we made a thousand pounds (20,000 shillings) on each bus we were making the full margin, giving nothing away. The secret was that I had done a deal with the Machakos Bus Company that they would buy them back at 20,000 shillings each and develop African bus operators in order to get into the market for the minor routes.

"A thousand pounds each, you say?" he mused, rolling his tongue in his mouth as if he were chewing a wasp, "Well, they'll be gone in two weeks - or you're sacked!"

The buses were gone in one week, I was not sacked and on rolled our juggernaut of success.

As an industry trained automotive engineer, I was time served more than most for my age due to learning from my early youth with my father and his collection of vintage and veteran cars and motor cycles. I'd been doing this from the age of ten and on one school holiday I forgot to hand pump oil into the crankcase of a 1914 Triumph motor cycle. Rather than get cross - and Father had a volatile temper - he said, "You seized it. If you want to ride it, you had better UN-seize it!"

It had been another lesson learned in basic motor engineering. It was also abundantly clear to me that careful driving was a major factor in the reliability of any motorised transport - especially in the African terrain.

Leyland were the first manufacturer to introduce fully air-braked trucks and buses. The vehicles were also fitted with an overdrive which meant that sixty miles per hour was achievable. What was happening was this: the drivers were using the efficiency of the air brakes with the full speed now available to them and literally setting fire to the brakes. Fortunately it was a simple task to remove the overdrive as it was outside the gearbox and took only twenty minutes to remove, which brought the speed down to forty miles per hour. Once this was done there were no further problems, although for a few months the drivers did complain about the lack of speed.

So I introduced an incentive with the sale of every vehicle: when they reached a hundred thousand miles with only regular servicing and maintenance I would present the driver with a 'gold' watch. I bought these from the local Omega/Tissot dealer for £15 each – they were a cheaper version of an Omega watch but under the Tissot brand - the price of which I had already added to the original sale price. It worked like a dream. Amazingly, our vehicles became much more reliable and more importantly, Leyland's reputation for reliability and service soared sky high. Every driver wanted his gold watch.

We had an ongoing production line which was turning out forty vehicles a month and I had spent many months working out how we could introduce total parts commonality. Upon my advice we cut down on the number of different parts and products we needed to keep in stock. We matched the new Leyland engine with the tried and tested Albion Clydesdale chassis, including the tried and tested Albion gear box and back axle, and settled on a modular chassis that we could adapt for all trucks and buses. By using the same major units in 90% of what we imported, it meant that if we didn't have a part in stock I could take one off the production line and replace it with one I could airfreight in the next day. This meant we were the only automotive supplier in East Africa who could guarantee to get any Leyland vehicle back on the road in 24 hours.

With this in mind it allowed me to make my boldest move yet, which was to take out a double page spread in both English speaking newspapers in East Africa, the East Africa Standard and the Daily Nation, proudly boasting that we could guarantee to get your truck or bus back on the road in 24 hours with a 100% parts cover. The opposition could only ever guarantee a 6 week turn around and I knew we could honour our claim.

But Ian Dall was not amused and I was called in to see him for the bollocking of my life. I hadn't told him about the adverts, you see. After carefully explaining to him how it worked, he broke out the Havana cigars and all was well! The orders came rolling in and I, of course, was soon talked about throughout the East African automotive market place.

Fraternizing with the opposition is not an activity I have ever condoned or got involved in. Any secrets you might glean are eroded by the secrets you give away after a glass or two, and my secrets were a lot better than anyone else's anyway. But there were certain haunts where the opposition gathered on Saturday lunchtimes after work to gloat - or to moan, more often than not. One of these was the Norfolk Hotel where you could enjoy the most exceptional curry in all of Nairobi. Standing behind a group of men at the bar, waiting my turn to be served, I heard one of the chaps in front of me turn to the group beside him and ask, "Have any of you lot ever met that bastard Bill Ford?" It was time for me to quietly drink up and disappear.

In the middle of 1962 we took the agency from Gailey and Roberts in Kampala, Uganda and in Dar Es Salaam where we bought new land on the airport road to build a branch for Leyland Albion Tanganyika. I stole the best salesman from D. T. Dobie who had the Mercedes franchise in East Africa. Colonel Dobie was the owner of Dobie's and my new recruit, who I appointed as manager, was an Ismaili Indian by the name of Ken Kassum. His family were the most prominent Indian family in Dar Es Salaam, his elder brother being a minister under Julius Nyerere. His father's house overlooked the entrance to the beautiful lagoon, which was absolutely spectacular. His next door neighbour's house belonged to Ali

Khan, black sheep of the family Aga Khan. Often Rita Hayworth would join him for holidays…

Ken was an exceptionally good businessman and he would join me in visiting customers in Tanganyika. We then started a production line in Dar Es Salaam which was very successful.

Each year all managers world wide, who had increased their revenues and targets by more than 10%, were given a 10% pay rise. Of those that hadn't achieved their targets 10% would be sacked. By the end of 1962 I was on a salary of over five times what I'd been getting back in England and I was about to get a pay rise equivalent to what my annual salary had been at Oscrofts only two years ago!

All the managers in East Africa were required to attend the 1962 end of year meeting in Nairobi as usual, where Donald Stokes and Sir Henry Spurrier were to announce some changes. The senior rep in East Africa was asked by Donald Stokes if he would take on the combined territories of Uganda, Tanganyika, and Kenya. I think Stokes knew the man would turn it down, which he did saying that it couldn't be done. I jumped at the chance and was offered the job.

I doubted it could be done properly if I did it the same way as I had when operating from Dar Es Salaam. But it could be done if I learned to fly and got a plane!

I started taking flying lessons immediately and I was allowed to fly solo within 8 hours. I absolutely loved it! It was a Piper Colt which was controlled entirely by a rudder & aerolons control, with no flaps and a fixed undercarriage. I took my first take-offs and landings in it and then graduated onto the forty odd exercises which were part of the pilot training. After a few hours this involved steep turns and on one of these steep turn manoeuvres there came a loud bang – one of the two exhaust manifolds had fallen off. At the Colt's normal engine speed of 2,200 revs per minute flames would have shot out and probably had the plane on fire within seconds, so I throttled back to 1,700 rpm. This caused popping back which was equally dangerous, so I increased the engine speed to 1,800 rpm which was just enough power to keep me up.

I called into Air Traffic Control with a May-Day call and they cleared the airfield which allowed me to do an extremely bumpy emergency landing. Bear in mind that this occurred when I'd only had approximately fifteen hours training which meant that I had been flying solo only for seven hours. Again, my engineering background came to my rescue and probably saved my life. My life would have ended On Fire!

After forty hours combination of training and flying solo I earned my pilot's licence at the first attempt and it was now necessary to decide from where to buy a plane. This boiled down to either me buying one, the company buying one or leasing one. I wrote to Donald Stokes as Ian Dall said it was well beyond his remit to authorise such a precedent. I detailed my proposal just as if I were selling a fleet of trucks, with return on investment, a tenfold increase in efficiency, bigger market share and a whole host of additional benefits running into two pages.

I received a lovely letter back:

Dear Bill,

Congratulations on getting your pilot's licence.

No! We will not buy you an aeroplane.

Therefore, I suggest you hire one.

Yours sincerely

Donald Stokes

So I did - I hire purchased one from United Dominions Trust. The Piper agency was owned by Wilkin Air Services whilst the Cessna agency was owned by Safari Air Services. I had become friendly with my instructor, Jerry Van Os, and told him I wanted to move up to a fixed wing Piper Comanche 250 with retractable undercarriage. Jerry quickly counselled me, as it was not suitable for a new pilot. He suggested that I bought a Cessna 182 Skylane which was a high wing, rather than a low wing, configuration. This was powered by a flat six continental engine with variable pitch propeller. It produced 230 BHP and had space for three passengers and the pilot. However, before testing it Jerry made me fly the Cessna 150 and then the 172, each for a couple of hours, before getting into the Skylane. I then had two hours training with Jerry as co-pilot. The problem with this was that the Skylane he was selling, very unusually, only had single controls, meaning that although he could tell me what to do, he had to leave the flying to me. But, after a couple of hours, I was deemed to be safe.

Coming in to land the difference in power and weight was considerable and my landing was quite bumpy. I remarked on this to Jerry and he said, "Don't worry Bill; any landing you walk away from is a good one!"

That afternoon, I took the Skylane up on my own and was amazed at its performance. I could see for at least a hundred and fifty miles and I could fly close to one hundred and sixty miles per hour, feeling relaxed and free as a bird. On my return I bought the plane from Jerry, thus beginning another exciting part of my African adventure.

However I wasn't able to experience such a relaxed state when flying her for my first few safaris. I had no control over the weather - it was the monsoon season and the radio was my eyes. The first time I flew down to Moshi from Nairobi, going over the saddle of Kilimanjaro, there was thick cloud for most of the way. I had to fly low over the rising ground around the foothills but left the turn too late and immediately flew into cloud. I was only two hundred feet above the ground. Fear froze me to the controls and I was incredibly lucky that I came out as suddenly as I went in. There's a book written about flying into cloud without the requisite IMC (Instrument Meteorological Conditions) training and it's called "Thirty Seconds to Live". If you can't fly on instruments then the minute you go into cloud you are blind! I returned to Nairobi much chastened but lived to tell another tale.

Having plucked up enough courage to keep on flying, it was only a week later that I again ran out of visibility, this time going to Mombasa from Nairobi. I had to fly under the cloud meaning I had no radio contact with Air Traffic Control (ATC). As far as they were concerned I may well have crashed and could be dead. I was following what was the only road for two hundred miles, when I saw a small strip of level grass verge and managed to land with a bit of a bounce and a bump. After finding a phone in a nearby hotel I called ATC to tell them I was safe. I stayed the night and after a couple of G & Ts found that my nerves had returned to calm. The next day the rains had stopped and I flew on to Mombasa.

Another incident, during my initiation into the African skies, was again in the monsoon season. I was about five minutes out of Mombasa, flying due south to Dar Es Salaam, when the monsoon struck again. I went down to fifty feet above the palm trees and decided to carry on. Approximately an hour's flying brought me to the mouth of the Tana River, the only thing I'd been able to recognise since leaving Mombasa, when the alternator belt broke. This meant that I had to turn the radio off and use it only for emergencies. I managed to get in touch with ATC to give my flight plan and was asked to confirm my height, direction and remaining fuel. I reported that I had approximately three hours of fuel and was flying fifty feet above the palm trees at approximately 140 mph.

The controller replied with a laugh, "As regards the fuel, you'll need every minute of it, dear boy!"

I continued to fly on pure adrenaline, turning the radio on every few minutes as ATC checked that I was still airborne. Suddenly the next message came, saying, "You're right on course. Do you know The New Africa Hotel? Turn on to heading 330 and you're seven miles from touch down at Dar Es Salaam."

I could see nothing but cloud and heavy rain was noisily hitting the windscreen. I saw the apron of the runway unfold beneath me. Anther bumpy landing ensued and again I was reminded of Jerry saying, "Any landing you walk away from..."

I walked up to the control tower to thank ATC for saving my life and as I shook the man's hand he grinned and replied, "All part of the service!"

When the monsoon season ended, flying became the real joy it truly is and every hour spent flying filled me with more and more confidence. I started to take a few risks and perhaps I was guilty of showing off a bit, too.

There had been a military coup on Zanzibar and a rebel force had taken over the government building. I took a friend out one Saturday afternoon after the news had broken in the papers and on filling out my flight plan I asked permission to fly over the island of Zanzibar. The same man was on duty at ATC and I asked," How close to Zanzibar can I fly?"

He replied, "It depends on the range of your guns, dear boy, but I would keep above 2,000 feet if I were you!"

The coup was reversed a week later. The troop ship SS Oxfordshire, carrying SBS style troops to other colonial regions, happened by and with true colonial diplomacy persuaded the rebels to give up their plans for government. British pomposity probably furthered the breakdown of colonial rule in Tanganyika as the captain of SS Oxfordshire belittled the president, Julius Nyerere, by asking him to inspect his troops the following day.

My career had also headed skywards and, having been promoted to Sales and Services Director of Leyland East Africa, I was the youngest overseas director of any Leyland company worldwide. The opening of our branch in Mombasa had given us the template to dispense with Gailey and Roberts as our importer and directly importing everything ourselves was saving us many tens of thousands of pounds per year.

During my time in Africa we had become Leyland's most profitable overseas company, pound for pound. I was now in line for even greater things and my successor Bill Ball, a friend of mine and a manager from Gailey and Roberts in Mwanza, wished to join Leyland Albion. Initially Ian Dall objected to the appointment of a Gailey and Roberts' man, but I eventually convinced him as I was looking for an escape to return to England. My fame had spread back home and Father and Tom Slater, both now in their sixties, were wanting me to return to the family business and I spoke about it to Donald Stokes.

But for this chapter in my story, I will end with the most foolhardy of my flying escapades:

The inimitable joy of flying, on a clear day, over the rivers, plains and forests of that vast and beautiful land, once absorbed, can never leave you. I was smitten and changed forever. Nothing has come close to that exhilaration since my days of flying. You can be three miles high with mountains in front of you, rivers below and in an instant you can pinpoint exactly where you are on the map. There's a heavenly place in that sky where you can see the two highest mountains in Africa at the same time: to your left Mount Kilimanjaro and to your right Mount Kenya, both with snow on their peaks. If you spread your arms wide you feel you can touch them both simultaneously. South of Kilimanjaro, flying low over the Serengeti, you can witness one of the greatest living spectacles on earth - the migration of millions of living beasts, all moving as one and with but one purpose. God is never more evident than He is in Africa, and you witness Him entirely when you're in the air.

There were times I took Maivis flying with me, on the good days we continued to share for a while after all the turmoil.

And yes, we did join the one, two and even three, Mile High Club, teaching her a thing or two as the earth rolled by beneath us.

But my greatest flying folly was this:

I was flying from Dar Es Salaam back to Nairobi with Bill Ball, when I asked him, "Shall we fly over the top of Kilimanjaro?"

"Go on then, I dare you!" he goaded.

A couple of technical details are needed here, dear reader. The Cessna 182 Skylane has a flight ceiling of 19,800 feet above sea level. Above this the air becomes too thin for the engine and the aerodynamics for safe flight are not possible. The engine cannot produce enough power and in a climb it will stall, ending in almost certain disaster. Remember a similar problem with the Albion truck at six thousand feet in Nairobi and its lack of power? Also, the human brain, being un-acclimatised to such rarefied air, will close down and render the body to which it belongs unconscious.

Mount Kilimanjaro is 19,540 feet high.

Up we went. The first fifteen thousand feet were a dream. But then we encountered the phenomenon of downdraft - due to the hot air rising from the Amboseli plains and meeting the cold air from the mountain top. The cold air, being heavier, created a downward air pressure which was forcing the Cessna into the mountainside. By 17,000 feet I couldn't even turn back - there was no choice but to continue upwards being driven ever closer to the mountain. I had her on full throttle yet our speed was dropping and at seventy miles per hour, in a climb like that, we would stall and crash within seconds. If I had tried to turn away I would have crashed and burned. I was now down to eighty miles an hour and still slowing. It was all I could do to hold the controls. I was almost standing upright to hold her on course. I glanced across at Bill and saw that he'd passed out.

At about 18,500 feet my angel of mercy, who seemed to be with me at those times in my life when I needed her most, came to my aid by causing the updraft phenomenon. This occurs when the hot air bursts through and takes you high above the mountain. We flew over the top at 21,500 feet, looking right down into the mouth of the crater at the top. The engine spluttered, I trimmed the wings and on we soared higher than the eagles.

There are lots of risks I should never have taken in Africa; some of them were not really of my making but were largely due to my ignorance and naivety. My safari experiences whilst driving ranged from being momentarily stranded amongst a pride of lions to being stuck in the mud between a mother elephant and her offspring, a hundred miles from anywhere with a broken spring.

There were many near misses in the air, some due to my blasé devil take the hindmost youthfulness – like flying from Nairobi without re-fuelling at Iringa because it is not necessary in good weather. But, as we approached Mbeya with Ken Kassum on board in the southern highlands, we ran into heavy rain. That was the first and only time I didn't bother to re-fuel. Mbeya is surrounded by mountain ranges and we had cloud beneath us and cloud above us with mountains to the right at over 11,000 feet. One of my only navigational aids was a small NDB which pointed to the beacon. Suddenly the needle went down and there was a tiny opening in the cloud right over the landing field. I cut the throttle to tick-over, pointed the nose down and allowed the airspeed indicator to go to 200 mph. We landed safely on the grass strip and taxied to the control centre by which time the small hole in the cloud had disappeared. It then rained heavily for the following 24 hours. I learned a lot that day - that one could have cost us our lives or at the very least my licence.

There was the time I took Sir Henry Spurrier on a flight and handed over the controls to him in mid air after he'd told me he'd been a World War One pilot but was not now licensed – he loved that one whilst flying over beautiful East Africa.

Sir Henry had fought in the First World War before the founding of the RAF and was an early member of the Royal Flying Corps. He was the founder of Leyland motors and was responsible for their hugely successful growth between the wars and afterwards up until his death from a brain tumour in the mid 1960s, not very long after I last saw him.

Then there were the risks I took breaking Donald Stokes' rules which could so easily have resulted in my dismissal.

And there were many more, far too many to mention, but I wouldn't have missed a single second of it for all the world.

Would I do it all again?

Probably...

★   ★   ★

"After a few hours this involved steep turns and on one of these steep turn manoeuvres there came a loud bang – one of the two exhaust manifolds had fallen off."

Part Three

Returning home 1965 – 1975

ClockTower-Leicester

There is nothing like returning to a place that remains
unchanged to find the ways in which you yourself have
altered.

Nelson Mandela

Chapter 11

Homeward Bound

By March of 1965 it had become clear to me that I had to address issues in my life that I had put aside. My business life was booming, for sure; I was twenty-eight years old with the best of my career ahead of me and I was already one of the top performers in my industry worldwide, my only limitation being one I'd set myself. But my family and domestic life was as good as non-existent. I hadn't spoken to Mother and Father for some time and my marriage to Maivis existed only as a convenience: the convenience of honouring a promise on my side and access to a certain status and social circle on hers. I had never been "unfaithful" to her in the legal sense, although there had been opportunities aplenty on my rise through the ranks in Africa and there'd been times when I'd nearly succumbed to others' charms. But increasingly, as I made friends and contacts along my way, I learned some truths about her life that I wish I'd known when I first met her.

I had become a drinking buddy of Paddy's in recent years and lately we'd shared confidences. Some of the things he told me about Maivis had me almost gasping in disbelief. Paddy, if you remember, was the airline pilot who had been at the hotel bar

181

with Maivis when I'd first met her after a flight to Mombasa. One of Paddy's revelations went something like this:

"Do you know Bill, if I'd have known how it was going to be with you two, I would have warned you off her. I mean, she was the ultimate good time girl and anyone's for the taking. I'd been there myself a good few times when she couldn't find anyone else – one of the hazards of being a pilot I guess..."

I'd always thought Paddy was one of the good time guys. I knew he was married and had a family in Entebbe, yet he seemed to be with a different woman whenever I saw him. He and Jerry Van Os together were like David Niven and Errol Flynn.

"At the time you tangled with her she was seeing other chaps, but you were the only one that wasn't married. You could say she saw you coming a mile off! Pardon the pun!"

Paddy laughed at his own joke before continuing, "You were her saviour, alright! You might have thought no one knew but it was bloody obvious old boy - and you were the one that got caught with it. I tell you, there were at least five blokes that had a lot to thank you for - probably more if the truth be known - me included! She's still got one or two on her coat tails now, you know..."

Paddy turned away as he noticed the look on my face and I think he felt he'd gone one revelation too far with that last one.

I'd always harboured the thought that the child wasn't mine, which is why I so easily made the bargain with her to have it adopted. A paternity suit would have been very untidy and may not have had the result anyone wanted. I did get on with her very well in those first few months, if you remember, but I'd never dreamt there'd been five others she was sharing her favours with.

In my mind our marriage was over from the moment Paddy spilled the beans. Saying nothing to Maivis, I just carried on as normal and I don't believe she suspected what I intended doing.

Her mother and father had emigrated to Australia in 1958. Her father had come to Africa from the Seychelles, joining up with foreign workers in the aforementioned Groundnut Scheme. After it all fell through he'd gone to work as a civil engineer in Australia. It had been pretty clear by the time they emigrated that the opportunities in colonial Africa, and the easy pickings that brought for many, were fading fast. Self rule had been sweeping through the third world since India's separation in 1947.

I, myself, was not immune to the threat of the changing state of affairs in Africa.

Apartheid in South Africa was gathering momentum and white Afrikaans supremacy rule was creating a polarised and threatening new order: the coloured man would be politically and sociologically downcast. Nelson Mandela had been imprisoned in the July of 1964 which, to my mind, signalled the watershed of change in that great continent.

When I'd arrived in Africa, at the very beginning of the '60s, my feelings about Mandela were much the same as the rest of western society – that he was a black terrorist-opportunist creating unrest in order to cash in on his certain popularity amongst his own ethnic peoples; this opinion being the fodder churned out by the world's media to serve the capitalist agenda of profit before people. I had been a capitalist soldier of fortune then, of course, so I was bound to toe that party line. But I have since completely changed my view. I now revere Mandela as one of the two greatest human beings who have lived in my lifetime; the other being Winston Churchill...

Now Paddy was a real man of the world in almost every way a man could be. He'd flown round most of it, made love on every continent if not quite every state and was very adept at fixing things; i.e. organising ways through sticky problems. Born with some of the same DNA that Willie van der Spek had been blessed with, if you know what I mean.

A couple of weeks after his shocking revelations about Maivis, I was with Paddy again - this time with Jerry Van Os - to ask for their advice on extricating myself from the marriage. Maivis was about to go off to visit her mother and father in Australia for an extended holiday. At the same time I was to visit home to talk to Father and Tom Slater - at their behest - about joining the family business. I was also negotiating with

Donald Stokes after informing him that Father and Tom Slater wanted me back. Sir Donald understood my dilemma but wanted me to stay with Leyland; he'd offered me the job of opening up in the USA to take on Dodge and General Motors. The package on offer was astounding..

"...and you can take your bloody plane with you!" he declared.

I'd led Maivis to believe that, depending on which way I decided to jump, I would get set up and send for her to join me, either in America or England.

"She'll be in Melbourne, you say?" asked Paddy. "Well, I know someone there who will do just about anything for money, but it'll cost you a pretty penny. So, here's the plan. As we know, and much to your cost, Maivis is game for a good time. This person is Eastern European; he was one of the sewer rats in the war and has set up business in Australia as a private detective. He's a rutting stag of a bloke and trust me when I tell you that girls fall over themselves to get at him. Give me the address where Maivis is staying and he'll find a way to take her out, buy her a meal and spend some time with her. On the second or third night he'll operate the sting. At the appropriate moment his hired photographers will burst into the room and you'll have the proof you need to move on. It'll cost four grand, two up front and two when you get the photos."

Paddy assured me he'd once arranged something similar for

someone else and it had worked like a dream. I did think the cost was a bit steep but, on balance, it would be worth it. Besides that, in Australia it was legal to enter someone's home to get evidence if a domestic crime was being committed - and adultery was against the law.

I flew back to England in June 1965 with mixed feelings, as I am sure you can imagine. Africa had been very good to me, but the times they were a-changing, as Bob Dylan's brilliant song and album of the day was ringing out loud and clear, and the world at large had really woken up after the long oppressive years caused by the war.

Father came to pick me up from Heathrow, on his own, without Mother. With a stern look on his face, he informed me, "I had a letter some time ago from a Mrs Grandcourt, who lives in Melbourne. She was asking for thirty thousand pounds (in 1965 currency!) so that you can have a divorce from her daughter. I met with her in London last week and she told me all about your situation. I have to say, her news didn't surprise me. You can never trust these foreigners you know - of course you know - you know to your cost. I sent her away with more than a flea in her ear. I told her that the wrath of the Almighty and the whole weight of the criminal law of blackmail, served by the most fearsome lawyers in Christendom, would descend upon her if she did not get out of the country and fast. A scourge on the earth if ever I saw one. Oh, yes, and I have something called diabetes, but it will be gone soon enough. Don't say anything about it to your mother."

He had arranged for me to see the family solicitor at Moss, Toone and Deane the following day and at the end of our meeting, partner Ken Brydson said:

"I want you to answer me one question. Have you ever committed adultery?"

Without hesitation, I replied, "No."

That of course was not true, but he needed me to deny it due to the divorce laws applicable in the UK at that time.

"That's what I needed to hear," he smiled as I gave him the photographs.

A few weeks later I received my decree nisi. I didn't have to attend court as it was heard in my absence. The judge remarked, on seeing the photographs, "I never thought a human body could achieve such astonishing flexibility!"

As I foretold, Dad and Tom did plead with me to join Ford and Slater. Donald Stokes, being a true gentleman in all his dealings, agreed with my decision to return to the fold. Moreover, he provided us with the exclusive Leyland territories of Nottinghamshire and Lincolnshire, along with their run down premises, in return for twenty percent of our share capital and for one of his directors to have a seat on our board.

I returned to the family business on a salary of five and a half thousand a year, with a pay rise every six months if targets were met, plus a fully funded car of my choice. To put that into perspective that was fifteen hundred pounds a year more than any other salary I'd ever received and equal to a hundred thousand pounds a year in 2017.

I was a bachelor again - I was twenty eight years old, earning a fortune, this was the swinging sixties and the pill was helping the world and the boys and girls in it, swing like crazy. I don't think I need to provide too much more detail here - best if you use your imagination…

★   ★   ★

XKR 7

AC Aceca-Bristol.

Pa's Workshop – 1946

… and so hold on when there is nothing in you
except the will which says to them: 'Hold on!'

From the poem If by Rudyard Kipling

Chapter 12

When Darkness Falls

When I'd met with Donald Stokes in England in March 1965 to negotiate my future, I had contacted Claire at her family home in Linlithgow, Scotland. I'd discovered she was single again after a disastrous marriage - she had met and married a Swiss man in 1961 shortly after I had left her on the boat bound for England. She never spoke much about it, all she ever said was: "He wasn't at all nice to me after we were married..."

We'd talked and she had helped me to make up my mind to return to England and rejoin the family business. My father and Tom Slater were very keen to have me and I had learned a thing or two about negotiation, so as well as the five and a half thousand a year salary – five hundred more than they had ever paid themselves – I had also negotiated to have an Aston Martin DB5 as my company car. I would have been happy with an E Type Jaguar but Uncle Ken thought that the technical layout of the E type was likely to 'damage my health'. Of course the Aston Martin was the car to have even then, with the James Bond franchise in full swing demonstrating the value of automobile product placement in blockbuster movies.

It was my second Aston Martin, as I had bought a very rare Aston Martin DB2 in Mombasa for eight hundred pounds from a senior airline captain of East African Airways.

After serving 3 months notice in Africa, I came back to England for good in June 1965 and Claire came down to stay for a few days at the Three Swans in Market Harborough. It was the same weekend that I was due to collect my new car and one of Ford and Slater's delivery drivers drove us down to the Aston Martin factory in Newport Pagnell.

In Dubonnet Rosso with a tan leather interior, the DB5 was one of the most stylish motor cars on the planet at the time. Imagine how this could turn a girl's heart! As we drove up the magnificent drive to The Stone House in my gleaming, brand new Aston Martin, I felt like a king and Claire was to be my queen...

After a month getting up to speed at Ford & Slater's head office in Leicester, I took up my role heading up Leyland – Albion - Scammell distribution in the Grimsby branch.

Claire got a job in Grimsby in the autumn and rented a flat there, insisting that we both lived independently. This made sense of course – I hadn't yet received my decree absolute and we didn't want any complications. I lived at The Wheatsheaf Hotel during the week, which was a mile from our branch, so that I could be at my desk as early as possible each morning. In my experience as a manager, especially a young one,

People and Places

Father, Jack Ford, leading the field in the 1952 London to Brighton vintage car and motorcycle rally riding a 1914 Triumph H Model on Madeira Drive, Brighton. Interesting to hear in the local news recently that the Triumph Factory in Hinkley, Leicestershire has opened a new visitor centre, I wonder if any of Jack's old bikes are in there...

Annual threshing at harvest time at The Stone House, Market Harborough in the 1950s Brilliant days...

"I've worked 7 days a week all my life you know!"
Well someone's got to do it!
Nigeria, Lagos, 1980, during a tea break.
I was head of Automotive division with 11,000 people reporting to me...

Beautiful car, beautiful girl.
Claire on the bonnet of my
Aston Martin DB6 in 1966
at Bonnytounside,
Linlithgow, near Edinburgh.

I gave this Aston a
rating of only
5 out of 10.
Sure, it was fast and
furious but it had an
experimental 325
brake horse power
engine, with high lift
cams and it was almost
undriveable in traffic.
I sold it in frustration
after only 15,000 miles
and 9 months.

Dad, leading the field again
with Mum as his passenger on
the London to Brighton run in
the 1950s. He's driving the
1902 MMC
(Motor Manufacturing
Company).
The car on the right was the
first car ever licensed in
Leicestershire and Rutland.
The car on the left is the
60 mph Mercedes.

Claire holding two year old Kerry and Mum holding our terrier pup on the drive of Blaby Hall in 1971. The 1300 GT Alfa Romeo was Claire's favourite.

Tim Sage, driving, and my father riding through Leicester on a contract for H. Epton & Sons in the 1950s.

Photo from the Leicester Mercury Tuesday 25th April 1978. The deed is done! The caption says, "The Mayor of Charnwood, Mr John Bradley, officially hands over the lease for the track between Loughborough and Rothley to the chairman of The Main Line Steam Trust, Mr Bill Ford, at the ceremony held at the Great Central Station, Loughborough. Also in the picture is the railway's president Lord Lanesborough.

1961 East Africa. Me with Standard Vanguard and Yana the dog. This car was the third worst car I ever owned. I had it for only three months then the bulk head snapped and it was written off. Not fit for African Roads. A disaster of a car.

Father with Henry Challand on Victoria travelling from Lincolnshire to Leicester hence the extra water. Kitted out for sucking water out of ditches 1950s.

Threshing at The Stone House in the 1960s Each year in July you can still see demonstrations of steam traction engines with threshing apparatus hooked up at Steam and Country Fairs around the UK.

Father outside the Stone House in 1965.
The Aston Martin DB5 DNR 700C in Dubonnet red with tan interior is still one of my 5 favourite cars. It had a 4 litre engine producing 282 brake horse power and I got 140 mph out of her going north up the A46 north of Leicester. I wish I'd have kept it - today's value is £400,000!

Quentin More posing with the stuffed stag just in front of the ha ha at the Stone House in 1966. The stag was shot by Sir Humphrey De Trafford in 1872.. De Trafford, of Trafford Park in Manchester fame had the house built a little before the stag met its end. De Trafford filed for bankruptcy in July 1907 and caused a scandal.

Me in Father's 1902 MMC pictured earlier.
I was 18 years old when this picture was taken and had just left Stowe School to start my apprenticeship at Vauxhall.
Value of this beauty today is upwards of £750,000.

Ariel view of Ford and Slater complex on Narborough Road South, Leicester in 1978.
It was a seven and three quarter acre site.
It was a green field site when we moved there in 1966, just a mile from the newly built
M1 motorway.
Today green fields still exist to the east, behind the complex, but everywhere else has become
very suburban. I wonder how much longer those meadows will stay green?

Ford & Slater's Gwendolen Road workshops in the late 1930s. The Vulcan truck pictured here was like the one I gouged my head on when I was 4 years old which led to me getting my cards for the first time. And the van leading the truck was like the one Charlie Rowell and I travelled in after the Coventry blitz.

18

19

Where the empire all began in 1928. The original premises in Stonebridge Street where Father and Tom Slater started after being made redundant and given only one hours notice. They worked 18 hours a day to make ends meet and make way for Uncle Ken to come into the business in the early 1930s.

The Workshop in Gwendolen Road where I first knew I wanted to become an Engine Engineer at the age of three and three quarters!

20

The AC Aceca – Bristol.
One of the best cars ever made!

Nearly the very best car I have ever owned. I gave it nine and a half out of ten, and it was only beaten by the 1973 Ferrari Dino. It had a 100 D2 6 cylinder Bristol engine which was designed to the 1930s BMW. The chassis was built by John Tojeiro and was a tubular space frame. It is renowned as one of the top ten cars in the world and had an aluminium body. I could regularly do 125 mph on many roads and in any driving conditions. A simply beautiful car to drive. I was just twenty years old when I bought this. Its value today is in the region of £125,000. I bought mine for around £1,500 in 1958.

21

22

23

24

I have always regretted what happened to the Stone House, it was a truly beautiful house.
My father sold it because he wanted to live in a Hall. But to my mind this was better than any Hall.
Tom Wheatcroft the builder, of Donington Park fame, bought it for the land, so he said,
because he could get planning permission to build houses. He said he would not
touch the house. Within two years it was razed to the ground.
He could not have done that today.

AC Ace Bristol outside White Sashes, in Great Glen; the only house Claire, I, Kerry and Jane ever lived in together. Claire died only a few months after this picture was taken.

25

That Ferrari Factor. The Ferrari Dino 246GT. The best car I have ever had on all fronts. Beautiful to look at and drive, it not only holds its value, it makes money as well. I bought it from Sytner's in Nottingham in 1973 for £5775 and sold it in 1990 for £100,000.

26

From the best to the worst! Almost. This is the car Ocscrofts gave me when I started with them in December 1957 after my time at Luton. A disaster of its time.

27

Father bought Mother a brand new Triumph Vitesse in 1962. It was the only car that could turn around almost in its own length. I don't think Mum drove more than a few miles in it.

28

29

Eddie Sanetra loved driving Father's Rolls Royce cars. We stayed with "Uncle Eddie" every year during the summer as I was growing up. He was more like a father to me. He was a truly lovely man. He and his wife - a friend of my mother's family, owned a guest house in North Berwick called Cragside.

30

My mother and my sister outside Cragside, North Berwick in December 1969. This was the weekend my father died. I had travelled up overnight at breakneck speed in my Aston Martin DB6. This was the only time father ever said that he loved me.

The last known photograph of my father, Jack (John) Ford and my mother together.
He lost more than half his body weight through diabetes, and would not take any medication because of his Christian Science beliefs. Yet, all he had to do, as we now know was change his diet..
He did achieve his ultimate ambition though and became the master of his own Hall..
Although he only lived there for a couple of years, and never really enjoyed Blaby Hall as he became ill before he moved there..

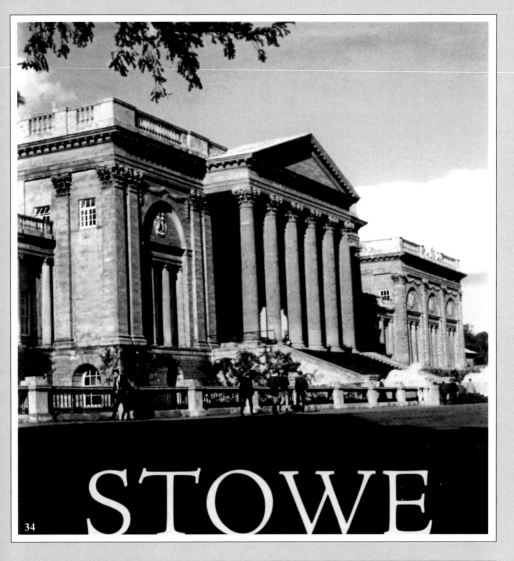

STOWE

What a place to go to school! I don't think I appreciated it at the time, who does?
I know now though how lucky I was to have received such a well rounded education.
I attended Stowe from September 1950 to June 1955.

Africa

I was confronted by this big boy on my way to work one morning!

This is why I learned to fly! My beloved SAAB 96 which I bought in 1962. I drove it for 3 years on roads like these and never had a jot of trouble with it. One of my top five cars of all time. A simply brilliant car.
This is the main road from Kisuma to Kericho on Lake Victoria, famous for its Brook Bond Tea plantations.

The RMS Carnarvon Castle.

I believed for more than 5 decades that I had done business with John Williamson, the founder of the diamond mines when I visited in Tanganyika (now Tanzania). Only when researching for this book did we discover that he had died 2 years before I ever went to Africa!

TO THE MEMORY OF
JOHN THOBURN WILLIAMSON
B. A., M.Sc., PhD., D. Sc.
BORN MONTFORT, QUEBEC 1907
DIED MWADUI 1958

DISCOVERER OF
THE MWADUI DIAMOND FIELDS
FOUNDER OF
WILLIAMSON DIAMONDS LIMITED

ERECTED BY
THE WILLIAMSON FAMILY

Just to prove I did it my way...
I bought my first Aston Martin - a DB2 -
out of my own earned money plus a loan
from a finance company in Mombasa in
1962. I bought it off a colleague whose
name was Tug Wilson.
It was a pretty poor relation to the modern
day Astons but nevertheless the start of a
great marque

Sunset over Lake Victoria - 1980
Farewell to Africa.
When I last visited on a family holiday in the 1990s I was saddened by how much had changed
since I left. Much the same as everywhere else perhaps...

Lord Lanesborough

The stories of the newspaper cuttings in the scrapbooks tell of his battle to save the GCR in the early sixties, fighting the minister of transport at every turn and getting support from councils and politicians to forward realistic bids to buy out the line; at times he had meetings with Beeching and Marples in person. All his efforts only delayed the inevitable, but that delay was crucial to allow time for people to gather and form the fledgling preservation movement; the offspring of that we now enjoy as our region's premier tourist attraction. If you think I am exaggerating as to how important all that delay was, just look at how fast they ripped up the rest of the GCR in the late sixties. Lord Lanesborough fought tirelessly at every stage and was present in all the dealings to wrestle for the land, permission, fundraising and financing of our heritage railway's formative years.

45

From big trains to little ones Lord Lanesborough loved them all

46

Leander Meander

Withdrawn at the end of steam in the 1960s, rescued in the 1970s and restored to full main line working order. David Clarke and I bought her in 1978 and ran her on Main Line duties and at the Severn Valley Railway.

Here she is, above, at the 1980 Rocket 150 celebrations with me on the foot plate - and below with a 13 coach train at Arnside in August 1979.

Top Left - attacking Lindal Bank near Ulverston in Cumbria Dec 29th 1979.
Top Right on Oldbury Viaduct on the Severn Valley Railway and bottom photo Sunday 7th September
1980 Leander at Bridgnorth on the Severn Valley Railway. This is the 10.30 departure –
first train of the day – Enthusiast Weekend.

Bridging the Gap

53

54

*February 12th 2016
The first sod was turned with Nicky Morgan, MP for Loughborough.*

Fame at last! BBC regional news aired the story.

Fame spreading…
This time we're announcing the ill fated museum project and the success in getting through the first round of funding with the heritage lottery commission.

57

As I said to Steve Johns as we were sorting through photos for the book - those who have known me in a managerial role will recognise me here in "Taz mode". Earlier in the day I'd checked down at the shed to make sure the engine was clean for the special announcement to be held at Leicester North with television, press and dignitaries.

It was filthy. I had to impress upon Fred Franklin - top left - that the Monday Crew had better get their act together and get the engine spotless! I'm afraid it took a "Taz" episode for the message to filter through...

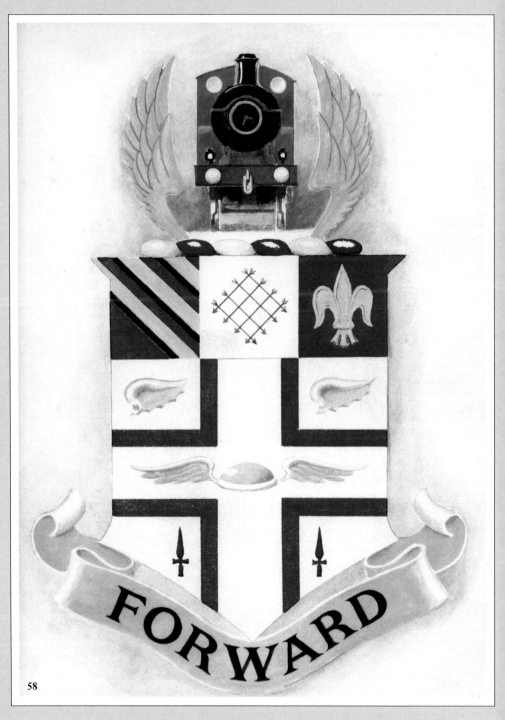

This is a scan of the original watercolour painting Lord Lanesborough had commissioned to
create the logo for what we now know as The Great Central Railway PLC
Every element in the picture depicts moving forward.
I whole heartedly hope this be so...

leading by example was always the most efficient way to raise standards.

The systems I inherited were ancient and grossly inefficient. Commerce in general back then was steeped in non-competitive price maintenance, monopolised markets and territory agreements which kept you tied to your area and all but forbade entrepreneurial thinking. Together with this, the motor trade had evolved using the theories put forward by Ron Sewell – the motor industry's training guru – who extolled the ethics of: 'The profit from your business comes from sales; the parts and service cover your overheads and costs.'

I totally disagreed with his theory and soon proved it to be wrong. In Africa I had turned this on its head. Tremendous rewards and profits could be reaped by focussing on the efficiency of servicing and increasing the stockholding of parts that you knew you would need. I knew that all I had to do to break free from those restrictive practices was to offer something no one else did. By Christmas I had started to experiment with a number of different systems, merging service with sales and introducing service schedules with fixed price servicing for all the vehicles. We were very quickly able to produce a service brochure to promote our new efficiencies. We also guaranteed to fix any fault on our repairs in 24 hours and offered a same day parts delivery service that was unheard of out in the wilds of the UK at that time in the heavy truck industry.

I bought our service manager a brand new Triumph 1300 and went out with him for several weeks visiting all our customers and potential customers with our new promo packs. It worked like a dream. I was replicating what I knew had worked in Africa, together with a few new ideas, and introducing it to the commercial vehicle market in England. It was a piece of cake really, once our customers tried this new service. It meant, however, that all management and staff would have to work at a much higher efficiency level. It was the start of our absolute involvement of apprentices which totally changed our ability to process work through the shop.

Ironically, today's situation in the motor trade has entirely changed; sales margins have been reduced, and difficult annual targets put in place. When these are reached margins are increased. Today the majority of the profit does come from service, parts and repair. But back then we were sweeping the market with our packages, mopping up deals, taking over the servicing of fleets and selling more new vehicles than had ever been known before. And after implementing new bonus schemes and incentives for more efficient working, our mechanics were the highest paid in the area and could earn double their salary via the bonus route. This also totally changed workshop efficiency as we could take on twice the amount of work previously booked in. In fact by having an apprentice work with each mechanic we had enough capability never to refuse work. To this day, this is a key issue to protect the future of any business and it is good to see that government and industry are now working along these lines; there's nothing new...

But, let me say at this point that the only way we achieved success was by team work; it is the golden rule in any business that you develop experts through on the job training who allow you to delegate with confidence. The more you delegate professionally the more time you have to focus on your profit centres and innovative ideas.

Having won the Lincoln and Nottinghamshire territories we embarked on a serious expansion scheme, opening one to two new branches every year. From 3 branches in 1965 we grew to 14 in 1973.

Each weekend Claire and I travelled back to Leicestershire where we stayed with Mother and Father at The Stone House. I know Father approved of Claire and Mother did too, of course. We had the most enjoyable time in those early months together, both of us found that we loved the leisurely things in life, such as canal walks and picnics in the countryside.

My father, Jack Ford, had strived to achieve his ambitions throughout his life, particularly the two main ones he'd formed as a child. If you remember he had been born into service with the very wealthy Gretton family at Stapleford Park. The Grettons were part owners of Bass, Ratcliffe and Gretton, famous brewers founded on the Trent at Burton on Trent. (In fact throughout the world, making beer is known as burtonising the water). Father's ancestors had been game keepers on various estates all the way back to the seventeen fifties and had never owned any property. Being constantly reminded, day after day, of his lowly position in the scheme of things, while the Lord and his family lived in a Hall and travelled in a Rolls Royce, Father had vowed then that he too would one day own a Hall and a Rolls Royce. In the event, he did much better than that. By the mid 1960s he'd achieved part of his dream by owning not only a brand new Rolls Royce but also several vintage ones, along with a whole host of other beautiful examples of motor vehicles from the glorious pioneering days of motor car development. Then, in 1967, he realised the second part of his dream by buying Blaby Hall.

There are always two sides to every human condition. Tenacity is the positive attribute that drives one forward to achieve, to succeed against the odds in many cases and it is the tow rope to hang on to when life's challenges get tough. The other, negative side to this is stubbornness. Dad had both of these facets in truckloads. He would never give up on his business, his ambitions, his friends, his family or his promises. And that certainly brought him riches far beyond his birthright. But his stubbornness in holding on to his beliefs undoubtedly shortened his life by a good decade. As a follower of the teachings of Christian Science he could not allow any medical intervention, unless it was a life threatening situation to the point where death would quickly follow. He'd been diagnosed with type 2 diabetes when he was in his early sixties. As a Christian Scientist he believed in the power of prayer; that God would heal all - as long as you believed and cast out fear. One of the main tenets of Christian Science is that if you cast out fear the body will heal, as it is fear that causes disease. He didn't know (or wouldn't believe) that all he had to do was change his diet. All we could do was watch as his weight diminished, over what turned out to be the last few years of his life.

There are a number of points I have pondered upon about faith and ambition. When Mother and Father moved into Blaby Hall in 1967, did his life begin to end with the realisation of his dreams? What part does ambition play in keeping one's clock of life wound up? When ambition fades do we then begin to lose that vital spark? I see evidence a-plenty all around me. When cancer strikes, does the end come sooner if the individual gives up all hope? When a partner dies and the bereaved is left hopeless and forlorn, all too often they soon follow. I look at the other side of this and see in my own life and experience how I have survived, sometimes against the odds. I know I've always had a positive outlook on life, feeling something driving me forward to better understanding so that I can get things right next time. Heroic tales abound in literature and in films; they seem miraculous and survival is inexplicable in many cases. Take the stories of those who emerged from the catastrophe of 9/11, or the heroes of war whose acts of faith seem beyond comprehension. It makes me wonder, in wonder sometimes. Maybe I can summarise thus: we stand a better chance of success, of survival and a longer life, if we look on the up side of any situation. Don't let thoughts of the worst that could prevail build a wall to stop us moving forward. But accept that walls will come along and our job is to build doors through them or paths around them.

After a successful eighteen months in Grimsby I was brought back to Leicester as Development Director. I had also been overseeing our Lincoln and Nottingham branches, implementing the same changes as I'd made in Grimsby. All three depots and service centres had been turned around and, pound for pound, were producing more return on investment than the rest of the group. Now it was Leicester's turn.

Claire came with me to my home town, securing a job as P.A. to the Managing Director of Fenwicks Department Store and, in the autumn of 1966, we were able to move in together at last, having bought a house at Houghton on the Hill.

Within weeks of my return to head office I introduced the same bonus scheme for our mechanics which I'd trialled at Grimsby. I'd learned from my days as an apprentice with General Motors that it was paramount to work out the time it took to do a job. By taking the average work rate for each job –

timing the slowest and the fastest - you get somewhere in the middle that you can call the standard. I had done this in Africa and then replicated it in Grimsby, Lincoln and Nottingham. Once you have this benchmark standard for each job you can fix the price for the customer and incentivise your workers based on how they perform against that benchmark. The better and more efficiently they work the more money they get in their pay-packet. The more efficiently the workshop runs the faster the jobs get turned around and the quicker the customers get their trucks back.

When I'd first arrived it was taking an average of three days for each major service; within three months we'd got this down to one day. Two other significant innovations I introduced in workshop practice within that first year were as follows: we recruited new apprentices, one for each mechanic. These new apprentices did all the fetching and carrying - if the mechanic was fitting brake pads, the apprentice would get the parts whilst the mechanic took out the old ones - and so on for every job. This alone speeded up each job by 30 to 40 percent. The second significant introduction was shift working. We had 100 service bays and an eight hour working day. Each bay had a fixed cost. Introduce another eight hour shift and you halve your fixed cost per job. Create 24 hour working, i.e. 3 shifts, and hey presto! You are making serious money as long as you can keep the work coming in. That bit was easy. Because our reputation for fast, efficient, fixed-cost servicing grew exponentially, the workflow increased parallel with that. In fact, we were so efficient we could take work in from other service dealers and still make good money. Our mechanics loved it, too. We increased their working day by half an hour to accommodate shift changeover so they all got a pay rise. Plus they were all earning mega bonuses and could rotate the shift which suited them the best. I had set in motion a trend for Ford and Slater that ran unabated for ten years. Profits doubled along with turnover and the years from 1965 to 1975 are without compare, neither before nor since, as the average profit year on year was 10% better than the last. Ford and Slater became the largest and most profitable truck dealer in the UK. But it is the way of the world and civilisations that once the competition finds out how you do something they copy it and take some of your share of the market. This is why innovation has to be at the core of every business, to strive to be one step ahead, to climb that little bit higher so you can see that little bit further. The graveyards of failed businesses are not filled with those that were always looking for new ways of working. Quite the contrary - look at who's at the top these days – Apple, Facebook, Microsoft, Google, Amazon, et al. You could say that their stock in trade is innovation and entrepreneurialism and the products they sell are just by-products of that. But Ford and Slater had a good ten year run at the top and you will see how we made the very best of our success.

My relationship with Claire blossomed with every season and even then I knew that those were the best days of my life. We married on March 30th 1968 and honeymooned on Lanzarote. Our first child was born in August 1969 - a daughter whom we named Kerry and we were blessed with a second daughter, Jane, in April 1972. But I couldn't even have imagined the tragedy and sadness that was to come.

There is the stuff of life to contend with, or, more to the point in this story, the end of a life, that impedes the best laid plans of mice and men. Father's diabetes was relentless and its outcome inevitable as he would take no advice nor receive any treatment. Diabetes had absorbed the life from him and at the time of his death on 20th November 1969, at the age of sixty seven years, he weighed just an ounce or two over five stone.

My mother had telephoned me in Leicester, as they were on a short holiday in North Berwick, saying that Father had collapsed. She was in tears, which was unusual, and I promised to drive up that evening. I went up on my own and this was one of the two occasions when I made the journey in less than four hours. By this time I had changed the DB5 for a DB6 Vantage fitted with an experimental engine, which was being developed for racing. I worked out afterwards that I had achieved an average speed of 78 mph - with no motorways or speed limits and at a time when the A1 went through all the major towns. Legally it's not possible today of course, as it meant driving between 130 to 140 miles per hour in many places, but I got there to find my father only semi-conscious. Before leaving Leicester I had bought him a bottle of mead as I knew this would briefly add to the sugar in his blood and give him temporary respite. The first sip or two was with a spoon, and he opened his eyes and recognised me.

The next morning I researched Christian Science hospitals and found there were only two in the UK, one being in Edinburgh. I drove there with my father who lay on the back seat of the Rolls with Uncle Eddie looking after him. We reached the hospital at about 7 pm and I carried Father, giving him a fireman's lift, up to the first floor where a Christian Science nurse, who was a trained SRN, took over - another angel I thought.

That evening, sitting alone with my father who was still conscious, I said, "Father, you know that I love you…"

"Do you?" he asked.

"Yes I do," I affirmed and he told me that he loved me, too. We both knew at that moment, I believe, that his end in this world would not be long in coming. Isn't it odd, that often it takes a situation at the very brink of life or death, before we dare to realise exactly how we feel about someone and more to the point, to be able to verbalise it? We should heed the old grandmother's wise words, "Don't leave it 'til I'm no longer there, don't leave it 'til you see my empty chair…"

This is why I tell all my children and grandchildren that I love them every time we speak. It has allowed me and mine to develop a really strong family.

On the 25 mile trip back to the hotel in North Berwick we stopped at a pub. Eddie and I had a couple of pints of beer - we both knew it wouldn't be long but we said little.

The next morning the telephone rang at ten to five. I answered it and the nurse said, "I am so sorry, your father has just slipped away." Apparently she had gone to see him around midnight and he'd opened his eyes and said, "What do you want me to do now?" She'd said, "Just rest and go to sleep." He'd smiled and slept. I'd known she was an angel - she was sent to look after my father on his final journey.

I put down the receiver and turned to see that Eddie and Jean's daughter, Katrina, had got up on hearing the phone. I fell into her arms and sobbed. We'd grown up together during my visits as a child and she was like a sister to me. I then had to break the news to my mother who had shut herself away and for all her Scottish stoicism she could not hold back the tears. We all huddled together: Eddie, Jean, Katrina, Mother and me. Even when you know the outcome beforehand and you have plenty of warning, it still hits you like a sledgehammer.

To my mind the first stage of grief, that first turn of the tap of your emotion, is the most profound and undisguised feeling that a human being can experience, next to abject fear. For a moment or two you are lost, without purpose or plan. Then instinct kicks in and what has to be done takes place. My sister Jacqueline arrived during the morning with her husband, giving rise to a second wielding of the sledgehammer.

My sister took Mother back home in the Silver Shadow, which had only done 5,000 miles. It had taken Father a year to clock that up, he'd been going blind over the last year, using his Land rover for trips to and from work, not wanting to have an incident in the Rolls. One day towards the end, he'd rung Mother from his office and asked her if the sun was shining. He'd looked out of the window and couldn't see much at all of a lovely cloudless summer's day

I arranged to fly Father's body back home. I remember meeting the plane at Donington airfield and that sledgehammer feeling smacked into my senses again.

Although he'd made a will, he'd made no provision to avoid any tax liability that would accrue at the point of his death. In 1969 death duty stood at forty percent of all assets. The total value of the estate was deemed to be in the region of £300,000 with the shares valued at two pounds per share of which Father owned 100,000. He had left his shares 50% to me and 50% to my mother with an equivalent amount in cash to my sister Jacqueline. The house was to go to Mother, the veteran vehicles to me and various other investments to Jacqueline. It had been assessed that we would have to find £127,000 to pay off the inheritance tax bill – nearly two million pounds in 2017. We were faced with the darkest of choices: to either sell the shares or all the material assets. We all agreed that the shares must be kept at all costs. So everything else, Blaby Hall, the collection of veteran vehicles, the traction engines, all had to be sold.

Mother had not had the best of decades dealing with my father through his illness; he had been, in some ways, a bit of a dictator who wouldn't listen to advice, especially about his health. In 1971, after the Hall was sold, the estate divided up and the death duties paid, she married a family friend, John Michie, and moved back to Scotland. Whilst travelling down for a holiday in 1976, Mother and her husband stopped off in Ilkley. They saw a cottage for sale, fell in love with it, and bought it there and then for cash.

Who knows what may have become of Mother had my father survived? But without him, she did as she pleased to a large extent, drank a bit too much of the hard stuff and in 1978 died in her sleep at the age of 71 from a massive heart attack, while my two girls were staying with her for a holiday. I had come to Ilkley to pick them up and knocked on the door at 6.30 in the morning. A red-eyed John Michie answered the door and said to me, "Your mother has died in her sleep."

I took Kerry and Jane back to Leicestershire the same day after helping the undertaker to lift my mother into the coffin. She had died in peace...

I was lost again in that maelstrom of sadness and unfairness of a loved one gone too soon, with a dent in our love that was left unmended. I never got the chance to tell Mother I loved her as I had told Father. We had spoken on the telephone the night before and the conversation had ended on a sour note. But I don't remember what we had argued about...

Ford and Slater continued to boom, however, with its growth unabated, while Tom Slater tried to manoeuvre me out of the company as he felt outnumbered without Father at the helm. Vic Jarvis, who'd been appointed a director at Ford and Slater at the same time as me in 1965, had always been Tom's man, taking his side in every dispute. There was an unconfirmed rumour that Vic was Tom's illegitimate son and the favouritism shown to him by Tom would always support the tale. He and I were often at loggerheads, at opposite ends of an opinion or a change in direction. He'd objected most fiercely to my idea of bringing together sales and marketing into the service operations and I often thought he was envious of me and my lifestyle. I recall one heated exchange we had when he taunted me with, "The way you live your life you'll be dead by the time you're forty – and then, when they've buried you, I'll dance on your grave!"

Not to be outdone, I retorted, "You're wrong, because when you die I'll have you cremated and your remains put in an egg timer, so that for the first time in your life you'll work for your living." That upset him.

That was the day I learned how to deal with Vic; he was very quick witted and I just had to match his wit each time. Thus began a better rapport between the two of us, we worked well thereafter and became firm friends, respecting each other for our different skills and talents.

But the 'favouritism' increased after my father died. I discovered that Tom's plan was to appoint himself as chairman instead of Uncle Ken, who was to retire at the age of 70 the following year, then he was going to appoint Vic as MD. Part of the agreement with Father, Tom and Ken, when I'd joined the board of Ford and Slater, was that no one would ever be promoted above me and that I would one day run the company. I confronted Tom in his office and called him, "A lying bastard!"

He rose from his chair, almost trembling with rage, but unable to get his words out fluently. He had suffered a stroke a year earlier which had left him with slightly slurred speech and slowed him down physically.

"Don't you be so cheeky!" he yelled at me as best as he could muster.

I made it plain that I knew what his plans were and that he should be ashamed of himself for contemplating such a breach of trust. He ended the altercation with, "I think it is better for all concerned if you were to leave the company!"

I said to him, "Grow up! We are both directors with similar share holdings and I am going nowhere."

I'd completely changed the fortunes of Ford & Slater and it would be Tom who would ask me back to Head Office to take over from him when he retired some three years later. I was already running group parts and service as well as development of the branches. Tom was a simply brilliant salesman and had done so much in the crucial development of Ford & Slater. What was wrong was, although he didn't wish to retire, in the 70's chairmen of PLCs had to retire at the age of seventy.

I have seen this predicament often in my life. Someone builds an enterprise, brings in rewards beyond imagination, takes all the risks and implements change successfully, only for someone in the wings to elbow out the champion and settle in the comfy chair that never belonged to them. You will read later in my story how this is often a recipe for swift retribution that can lead to disaster for many if not all...

But to go back to 1965. Along with my appointment as director, our appointment as sole distributor in the counties of Lincolnshire and Nottinghamshire was added to our existing territories for Leyland trucks and Leyland had received a 20% shareholding in the Ford & Slater group. As was prudent and customary, Leyland had put one of their professional directors on our board. This was David Abell and he and I had soon become good friends, trusting each other implicitly in all our dealings. He knew what was happening and I had already contacted Edgar Byass, senior partner of Moss Toone and Deane, upon leaving Tom Slater's office after the row. I was the one who dealt with all legal matters between customers and solicitors and I asked if they would act for me, against the company if necessary. Edgar Byass then told me to go to the next day's board meeting and under no circumstances was I to resign. If the current chairman wished to resign, I was to try and stop it. If that was not possible I was to say that I was unable to attend that board meeting; I was to leave and immediately give him, Edgar, a ring.

You can imagine my lack of sleep that night. I saw David Abell go into Tom's office before the board meeting for his customary cup of coffee. The board meeting proper then started on time at 11 am. Chairman Ken duly gave a talk on how much fitter Tom Slater would be for the role of chairman and that it was better for him to take over the chair. I told the board that I thought the current chairman was doing an excellent job and that I was happy with him; I had been unaware as to what was going on until the day before and I felt that any decision should not be rushed but be put into the next board meeting. To my amazement David Abell said that he had been unaware of this coming up until an hour ago and that any decision should be delayed for a month.

Our combined shareholding and the support of my mother meant the decision could not be taken and it was duly postponed.

It was almost a year later that David told me that he had said to Tom that he and Leyland did not think Vic was capable. In the meantime, I had negotiated with Vic Jarvis that we become joint managing directors with Tom as chairman until he retired. Then Vic would take over as chairman and I would run the company as sole managing director, which would include sales and markcting.

At the ensuing board meeting, held the following month, this was unanimously passed. Vic and I had, of course, told Tom of our agreement and he was totally on side with it.

★   ★   ★

*"First, the industry must be of a size and pattern suited to
modern conditions and prospects. In particular, the
railway system must be modelled to meet current needs,
and the modernisation plan must be adapted to this new
shape and with the premise that the railways should be run
as a profitable business."*

Foreword of the Beeching Report written by Prime
Minister Harold Macmillan - 1960

Chapter 13

Trains and Boats and Planes

Prospects for a business serving the growing road transport industry in the United Kingdom in the decade and a half from 1960 onwards had never been better nor ever would be again. Automobiles became king with the building of the motorways and the shutting down of thousands of miles of "unprofitable" railway routes; this fell perfectly for Ford & Slater, especially with me soon to be in the driving seat.

I have always felt that Harold Macmillan's words "modelled to meet current needs" was dictated by Ernest Marples as he sat by Macmillan's side with a pistol cocked and aimed square at his head until he'd finished writing. Ernest Marples was not only Minister for Transport but also the Managing Director of Marples Ridgeway, a civil engineering company specialising in motorway construction. A clear conflict of interest of course but what the heck! This was the 1960s when 'anything goes' wasn't it? Marples was forced to sell his shares eventually and he did comply - by selling them to his wife!

But I digress and it would be most disingenuous of me to be overly cynical. I have an awful lot to thank the conservative governments of the 1960s for, as you have read. Ford and Slater boomed during this era and you could say that for every mile of motorway Marples built, Ford and Slater sold another truck and with every truck came another service contract and all the parts that that entailed. And, I don't say this glibly, one of our major customers was Hoveringham Gravels who supplied road stone and dressings for tarmac road surfacing materials who sold to Marples Ridgeway, and at the zenith of that relationship we were supplying 400 trucks every year just to them. In addition, it was Doctor Beeching's recommendation to close the Great Central Railway, among others, which led to my 40 plus year involvement with that great railway as a heritage enterprise.

I could also say that for every hundred or so miles of motorway built we opened another branch of Ford and Slater, until by 1973 we had 14 branches.

This gave us a territory from the Humber to the Wash, South to Ipswich across East Anglia and then across to Oxford and south to Aylesbury and up to Coventry and back to Leicester.

By 1967, when I was firmly in the driving seat of everything except sales we were opening and developing branches and visiting every branch twice a month.

In 1966 I had taken my English Pilots' licence and I joined the Leicester Aero Club, based at Stoughton, just a stone's throw from the house Claire and I had bought in Houghton on the Hill and only a fifteen minute drive from Ford and Slater on Narborough Road, Leicester. There I made a close friend in

Michael Goddard. Michael's family had been business people for a generation or two longer than mine; his great-grandfather had been a chemist, labouring long and hard in his search for the perfect formula to safely clean silverware. In 1830 he patented his formula and the name Goddard became synonymous with the polish that is still sold today, renowned as the best there is for the job it was invented to do. Michael though, like me, was a businessman working hard in all his dealings. His father had been Lord Mayor of Leicester in 1953 and the family owned The Imperial Typewriter Company which was sold to Litten industries in the 1950s. Michael worked his way up to become a director of Wadkin Machinery, the world famous woodworking machinery company set up in the late 19th century. The business had come into the Goddard family in 1912 because the owner at that time, a certain Mr Denzil Jarvis - Wadkin's original partner, had drowned on RMS Titanic whilst on a sales trip to the USA. Wadkin Machinery had been sold to the Goddard family by Mr Jarvis's widow who was a family friend.

Michael's father, Holland Goddard the 1953 Lord Mayor of Leicester was knighted by the Queen, as were all Lord Mayors of that year.

Throughout my life I have been drawn to fixing and mending things and it is in my enduring nature not to let an opportunity pass me by, even if the cost might outweigh the reward. The Leicester Aero club was being run by a bunch of amateurs who hadn't kept an eye on the pounds or the pennies and by the time Michael and I had become friends, it looked like it was going to be wound up. Any assets, including the aircraft and the land, would revert back to the Co-op; they would build houses on it and there'd be no more facilities for flying enthusiasts in or near Leicester. Furthermore it appeared that a small group of members were attempting to acquire the remains of the club on the cheap without going through the proper consultation process. I knew straight away that this was wrong and advice from Ken Byass, Ford and Slater's trusty solicitor, was needed. I had asked Michael if he would be willing to come in as a partner with me to rescue the club and we'd agreed to invest five thousand pounds each. On the advice of Ken Byass we arranged a consultation with counsel at Lincoln's Inn Field in London. The group of members, who thought they'd succeeded in buying the assets, had not waited for the entity of the Aero Club to be wound up properly and therefore their acquisition was deemed unlawful and was reversed. A meeting was arranged between all interested parties and the proposal that Michael and I had put forward was accepted, regrettably by some, I'm sure. But we had the legal argument in our favour as well as the majority of the rest of the membership on our side. We brought in one other director to complete the process: Michael Turnor of Montague Turnor Estate Agents. Michael Goddard was elected as chairman and I was secretary. He stayed on for many years afterwards and was a tremendous help in developing the club. Together we set about transforming the activities of the club: holding open days, pleasure flights and galas which promoted the club with great success.

Of course there were others who also helped Leicester Aero Club to become one of the top clubs in the country: Jerry Van Os, my dear friend since my African days had left Africa, like most colonialists, and taken the splendid job of CEO of Cessna Europe based in Brussels. We obtained a Cessna agency which proved profitable at the time. For our annual air days Jerry would bring in up to six demonstration aircraft and one year he brought the top of the Cessna executive range: the nine seater Cessna 421. With it came his chief pilot, Jim Dale, a Texan with 36.000 hours flying experience. Jim had done his main proving in the polar regions with the inimitable B29 which is still flying in the USA today. If he had been ten years younger he would definitely have been in the NASA team of astronauts. At the air day he flew at a hundred feet above the runway in the 421 with one engine feathered and barrel rolled it. The 421 had no negative 'G' and any manoeuvre which produced it would have folded the wings. He also flew our one aerobatic plane in the Cessna range the Cessna 152 – what a display he gave! This helped with the acquisition and loan of aircraft when needed. Then there was our chief flying instructor Joe Sharps, a great leader of men and again one of the best pilots I have ever met. His dare devil stunts on our show days I don't think have ever been rivalled; he could loop the loop, bottoming out within ten feet of the ground. It wouldn't be allowed today. He went on to be a senior pilot flying long haul Boeing 707s and thereafter jumbo jets. One other who I would like to introduce here is Tony Moy. He was singly responsible for pulling all the threads together, managing all the logistics and promotion involved for our world renowned 'Air Shows'. Thousands attended from all over and I still catch a conversation now and then about the planes and sights to be seen in our little patch of South Leicester sky. Tony was a self made man. He'd joined the Metal Box Company as a trainee straight from school, worked himself up the management ladder and then left with a colleague to set up what became the world famous travel company Page and Moy. He was, without doubt, the most accomplished marketing man I have ever met.

When he sold Page and Moy in 1998 he became a highly respected Formula One commentator as well as commentating on US car racing circuits and at many other sporting events throughout the world. He died in 2016, and there were hundreds at his funeral in Great Bowden, Market Harborough, Unfortunately we had lost touch and I only found out he had died whilst we were researching for this book; it took me a few weeks to come to terms with this news.

From my experience in all of this, I learned very quickly that in any members club, the members will shower their benefactors and saviours with almost unlimited gratitude until the situation has stabilised and all is on a forward path. It is then that everyone suddenly knows how to run things better than you do.

Ford and Slater's rise was meteoric and we were increasing turnover and profit 10% year on year so I bowed out of the Aero Club, giving my investment in it to the club and leaving it in a far better state than anyone could have imagined when I'd first arrived.

I expect you'll be wondering what I turned to next? I can't explain the why or the wherefore of my entrepreneurial spirit, it is just there within me. Certainly a large part of it is recognising that something could be done better; trying and experimenting to prove a theory from my experience and having the wherewithal to do it - or more to the point, creating it.

When Claire had first moved down to Leicestershire and we began spending weekends together, we especially enjoyed our own company breathing in country air whenever we could. We took long walks along the canals around Market Harborough, of which there were miles and miles. We both led such busy lives during the week we really did appreciate the term "a breath of fresh air".

Many a time we started and finished our walk at the marina, where we had come to know the owners of Harborough

Marine. And, as way follows way, we bought a forty foot narrow boat from them for four thousand pounds. That pace of travel is just made for peace and tranquillity: the gentle throb of the diesel engine nudging you along at walking pace, hardly rippling the water or causing a splash so no wildlife need panic to move out of your way, is the closest thing to heaven I have ever known, especially with the most beautiful girl I could ever dream of by my side. We could escape into an almost isolated world, mooring down water from some idyllic pub that we could call our own for the evening. We'd light our little log burning stove to take the chill off the night and spend hours in each others arms, all our cares drifting away with the wood smoke, to pick up on another day, if needs must.

I remember a long weekend we spent at Trevor near Llangollen, North Wales as our base, which was Harborough Marine's other centre. Looking westwards while traversing the Pontcysyllte Aqueduct you are flying without wings at three miles an hour, a hundred feet above the majestic wooded valley of the river Dee. I imagined that was how an eagle feels, soaring on the thermals on a summer's afternoon. Bliss!

But my mind had turned again and on the way back I guess I didn't say much, I was too busy planning my next venture.

I spoke to Tony Moy, whose fiancée was an absolutely stunning girl called Judy; a talented chef as well as the owner of a number of high class dress shops, one of which was in Market Harborough. She had previously worked as a chef on hotel boats and Tony had been introduced to the delights of canal cruising by her.

Harborough Marine, owned and operated by the Baker Brothers, built thirty new boats a year; they sold twenty and kept the other ten to build up their fleet of hire boats which were the best boats in the business. Tony Moy and I set up a company with a fifty – fifty stake and bought six boats over the first year. We moored them at Wooten Wawen near Stratford on Avon, Market Harborough, Trevor (Llangollen), Great Heywood near Stafford and Aynho in Oxfordshire. We took out a series of small adverts in the Sunday papers and the business took off like a dream. The Baker brothers however, were struggling to make ends meet and asked if Tony and I could buy a share in their business. We agreed and bought 25% of the business each; we joined Anglo Welsh Narrow Boats and prospered even further, becoming the largest supplier and hirer of narrow boats in the UK.

But the structure of the company was such that there was always a state of armed neutrality with the Baker Brothers on one side and Tony and I on the other; the slightest difference of opinion could shake the tense alliance into destruction and it was clear that one of us had to leave. I thoroughly enjoyed my foray into the boating world, but with my father's illness and the relentless pace of growth at Ford and Slater it was best for me to sell my share in the company. I sold to Page and

Moy, who in turn bought out the Baker Brothers. Eventually Anglo Welsh Narrow Boats was sold to a third party and everyone who'd been involved made a handsome profit.

★　　★　　★

When my son, Ian, was at university, we had a wonderful time, spending some weeks of a summer vacation on Stella Maria. We explored the waterways around the Potteries and the Black Country and discovered some lovely things...

If suddenly

you forget me

do not look for me,

for I shall already have forgotten you

But

if each day,

each hour,

you feel that you are destined for me

with implacable sweetness,

if each day a flower

climbs up to your lips to seek me,

ah my love, ah my own,

in me all that fire is repeated,

in me nothing is extinguished or

forgotten,

my love feeds on your love, beloved,

and as long as you live it will be in your

arms

without leaving mine.

From the poem If You Forget Me by

Pablo Neruda

Chapter 14

Forget Me Not

In 1967 we had the shares of Ford and Slater valued at twenty seven shillings and six pence a share, although we were a private company and it was very difficult to be accurate with a valuation. There were three hundred thousand shares split between six of us, but not equally. When my father died in November 1969 we had to ask the Inland Revenue to determine a value for death duties and the figure they suggested was two pounds per share. Tom, Ken and Vic Jarvis baulked at this and were all set to argue the case with the tax people as at this valuation it could mean that they each could accrue a greater personal tax liability. Any dispute would have led to an independent valuation by experts and all parties would be bound by their findings. I spoke with David Abell, whose opinion I completely respected in all matters to do with business.

"Take a close look, Bill, at your latest set of management accounts and tell me what you see. What is your net profit grossed up per year?"

I don't remember now the exact amount but I know Tom Slater had a go at me for "poking my nose into things that should be left well alone!"

I asked him what he meant by that and he declared, "We can't let people know how much profit we're making, they'll all want more from us!"

My reply to him was, "Tom, last year you, Ken and Father bought yourselves brand new Rolls Royce motor cars, I have an Aston Martin Vantage and Vic has a Bentley; it's pretty bloody obvious we're making a sizable profit! How much exactly is neither here nor there to the average onlooker and besides that, because of that healthy profit, everyone who works for us and docs business with us knows we offer security of employment and we are a hundred per cent credit worthy. Our customers know we offer the best value there is in the market. Therefore, the fact that we make a healthy profit is in everyone's interest."

As was becoming more usual these days, Tom left me to it, shaking his head in resignation while muttering something inaudible under his breath.

David Abell had gone on to say, "Multiply that profit figure by five or six, then add that to your net assets from last year's balance sheet and that's what your business is worth. Divide that by the number of shares and there you have it. What is that figure?"

Now these were the days before electronic calculators and a minute or two was required to work this out long hand. I was astonished at the result, "If I take it at five times the profit, it works out at twelve pounds per share!"

David smiled, "You'd better be quick and snap the Inland Revenue's hands off before they change their minds! If you don't take their offer of two pounds a share you'll owe forty percent of an additional four hundred thousand pounds and that would bankrupt the lot of us!"

After I had told this to Tom, Ken and the others, all was quiet on that front.

This stark realisation, I believe, swayed many of the decisions I took over the coming years. Apart from David Abell, none of us had realised the value of our shareholdings.

In 1969/70 there was no National Lottery but there were the Football Pools and the aim in those days was to forecast eight score draws with no one to share it with. Rather like a big win on today's lottery, it was beyond one's wildest dreams and picking out eight draws could bring you something in the region of a quarter to a half a million pounds. Each one of us had this value in our shareholding and Father's liability to the tax man was somewhere in the Pool's winner's ballpark.

I'm not sure exactly the moment we decided to float the company on the Stock Exchange and take Ford and Slater into Public Limited ownership, but I'm sure it was after we had settled with the tax man.

I know that during this time I was not the ideal husband. I was nearly always at work and when I wasn't my mind was on work, so I must have become a bit of a bore to Claire. She was a terrific mother to our firstborn Kerry, born in the year my father died. I'm so glad he got to rock her in his arms and I know he was very proud of her. Babies can melt the coldest hearts... But as I've said, Father did struggle with life during his last months and it was a very hard road he chose to tread in his final days.

Claire and I had shared a long journey in many ways. I first knew of her in 1960, from the photograph shown to me by Quentin More and Chris in Nairobi when I was twenty two years old. I don't know enough about love to say for sure that you can fall in love with a photograph, or fall in love at first sight, but it certainly felt like that. I've since regretted playing the perfect gentleman during those first days which I contrived to spend with her on the boat from Mombasa to Beira. At the time all I wanted to do was give her all of me so she would give me all of her and I know now that she wanted the same.

But, after I left the boat, she had a brief affair with a man who was not a gentleman; he took advantage of her and she was too ashamed of herself to tell anyone about it until she told me years afterwards, after we had returned to England. If I had behaved in that way, if we'd done as our instincts were urging, what would have become of us? Who can tell? In her presence I was in awe of her beauty, not just physically, but in a divine almost spiritual way, too. You may remember that I said she was a Quaker or, to be more precise, a member of The Religious Society of Friends? She was a quiet person, as her order preferred, acting rather than speaking. We never argued, ever, but we had our differences right from the start. She never got used to the ways of business and could never tolerate a lie. On one occasion, travelling from one appointment and late for another – how I so hate to be late! – I was caught for speeding and summonsed to either pay the fine and get an endorsement or appear in court and plead mitigation or innocence. I spoke to our solicitors asking what the chances were of getting off. It was a capable senior partner who asked me a pertinent question: "Is your speedometer reliable, Mr Ford?"

At the magistrates hearing, I apologised most sincerely, explaining that my speedometer was inaccurate so I was unaware of the actual speed I was doing. I'd taken a letter with me from Aston Martin stating that they could not guarantee the accuracy of my speedometer below 100 miles per hour. My solicitor argued the case further on my behalf. Before the case took place he went to see the magistrates' solicitor, who was there to give advice, telling him what he was going to base his case on and quoting a reference from a legal journal. I was to plead guilty with extenuating circumstances.

The two magistrates cleared the court and when we were called back they said that they were taking an unusual decision for the first time in that court. I had pleaded guilty and therefore I was fined £8 for the offence but with no endorsement. Previous cases were quoted of this occurrence where the defendant had been let off with just a fine. This is no longer a defence as it is now deemed the driver's responsibility to make sure he or she has the means to know what speed they're doing; no doubt as a result of the hundreds of well heeled motorists like me, along with their solicitors, pleading their innocence because the speedo' was bust!

Claire asked me when I got home that evening, "How did the court case go?"

"No endorsement," I replied, "I got off with just a fine."

"How? Surely it's an automatic endorsement for such an offence."

"I told them my speedo' wasn't working properly and they believed me."

"You mean you lied?" her look was accusatory, like a mother scolding a naughty child. She didn't speak to me for a week after that.

Shortly after we first got engaged in 1967, we talked about what we both wanted from our lives together. Of course, I was set for a life in business, seeing no reason to deviate from that, but Claire saw every reason to take a different path. She stated her case without contention, declaring, "Business isn't fair, is it? It's full of trickery and deceit as far as I can see. There is a better way, I'm sure of that."

It was as if there was nothing more to say and certainly no room for me to contest. She'd seen a feature in the Sunday paper about some people who had emigrated to New Zealand and started up a farm growing oranges and she suggested that we could do the same. I said to her that I could turn my hand to many things but I doubted I could ever turn a profit out of growing oranges. We didn't have anything more to say on the matter but she went on an extended period of silence while I got on with changing the world through Ford and Slater.

One day I came home and she'd left. A note told me she had gone to visit her sister Sonja and her husband who was in the U.S security forces stationed at Bremerhaven, in Germany. After a week I went to Germany and knocked on their door; it was opened by Sonja's husband who, not knowing who I was, asked me what I wanted.

"I have come to take my fiancée back to England."

There were many things we didn't see in the same way but there was one thing for sure that we did and that was how we resolved our differences: we each gave the other our all and everything was better.

But, to go back to business, by the middle of 1971 the dust had truly settled and we were making plans to take the company public. We created another tranche of shares, diluting our total ownership after the floatation by about 45% but almost doubling the equity in the company. This meant that we would still maintain control but would realise a considerable amount each for the share we were giving up. There were many hoops to jump through and obstacles to overcome and the due diligence was mind boggling; it was also very expensive as we needed an army of professionals to draw up all the proofs of compliance. But we did it and our success seemed to know no bounds. We had the very best financial director I have ever met in Don Kendall. It was Don who did most of the work on the public issue, and I offered to promote him to MD of Ford & Slater. He declined due to the stress involved and I spoke to my friend David Clarke who employed him. Don subsequently left the motor industry behind and became a director of Clarkes boxes where he was responsible for their public issue, raising money from National Westminster Bank.

Our turnover per annum at the point of going public was over thirty six million pounds, which made us the largest independent truck business in the UK and we were by far the most profitable with a return on investment of 16.1% - over a million a year. Imagine an investment like that today where you invest a thousand pounds and every year you would get one hundred and sixty one pounds back!

Life became a little more ordered after the floatation and I was able to spend more time at home. By the autumn, Claire was pregnant with our second child and we entered what was perhaps our most contented time together. Then in early 1972 Tom retired leaving Vic as Chairman with me as MD running the group and David Abell in full support. I was still busy, but I'd learned the art of delegation and the business was running like a well oiled machine.

I was also busy outside of Ford and Slater not only with Anglo Welsh Narrow Boats Ltd. but a new air taxi venture that I had started. After leaving Leicester Aero Club., I set up Donington Aviation which provided a service for businessmen. I'd bought two new Piper Aztecs, an older Piper Apache, a Cessna Centreline thrust 337 and wet leased a Cessna 421. It succeeded from day one and I flew many times from East Midlands Airport in our own private planes. Soon afterwards, in 1973, Michael Goddard joined me in buying a new Cessna turbo-charged 310Q so that Wadkins, his company, could fly their people longer distances.

On 6th April 1972 Jane, our second daughter, was born. Healthy and brimming with life, she added a new dimension to our own lives and it seemed that Claire's cup of happiness was as full as she could ever have wanted. She really was more than a mother to our two girls; even at that young age they seemed to be such good friends. It was amazing to witness the magical bond between Claire and her young daughters. To me, looking from the outside in, it was as if her whole life had been destined to come to this point - this is what her life was all about.

I had learned from Claire that Quakers don't have a hierarchical structure to their worship. They have no leaders and all are deemed equal with one another. There are no set rules to abide by as in other forms of Christianity and they don't believe in the traditional heaven and hell or that we will be punished for our sins. They believe we each know the difference between good and bad and if we do wrong we put it right through atonement and learning. Every human being is blessed by God and the main purpose of each of us is to do good and what is right by and for each other. The hereafter - what happens after we die - is what we leave behind; it is the good we have done in our lives and the children who succeed us that live on after we are gone.

I accepted that she didn't hold with my capitalist ideals, but I did question how it was that some of the greatest and most successful companies were founded and owned by Quakers, growing vast business empires and still holding on to their firm beliefs – Cadbury's, Lloyds Bank, Quaker Oats, Rowntrees, Bryant & May, Clarks Shoes and Fry's Chocolate – to name but a few. She would shrug her shoulders and say something along the lines of, "That was their way of doing good in their world. If you look at what they've left behind and their generosity to human kind, you will see what a great legacy they have bestowed. But it is not for me, I don't have that gift. You do Bill, but you're not a Quaker and I don't know what will become of us if you carry on working like you do."

We agreed to differ...

It was later that year, just before Christmas, when we received devastating news - Claire had breast cancer. In January 1973 she had a mastectomy.

"Was this some sort of atonement?" I asked myself.

Was it me or was it Claire who was to atone? The questions came and came but there were no answers. We got on with life and, as you will no doubt guess, I remained positive and urged Claire to do the same.

After the operation, when she was feeling a little better, we took a holiday and flew to Durban in South Africa to stay with her mother and Quentin her stepfather. Everyone tried to be jolly, making an effort to enjoy each others company and we did have some fun reminiscing about our early days on that most magical of continents. It was awkward for us all when we went to the beach, but no one said anything. Claire had loved to soak up the sun and she'd looked stunning in a bikini, turning heads where ever she walked. I'm sure many people had thought she actually was Claire Bloom. But not any more...

It's hard to remember now how that Bill Ford was thinking then. Hindsight distorts thoughts and memories because it knows what came after. The 'me' back then didn't know or, more to the point, couldn't know what was to come; carrying on as if life were constant and this was just another battle to fight, another wall to find a door in or a path to get around.

We celebrated Jane's first birthday on April 6th on the 747 flying back from Durban.

When we got home Claire began a course of chemotherapy. I was with her as often as I could be, taking and fetching her in and out of hospital for treatment. These were pioneering days in cancer treatment and I did think at the time – and have since – that we hadn't really come all that far in medicine in dealing with such a life threatening disease as cancer. Chemotherapy seemed to be the 1970's equivalent of the scalding hot baths they had used to treat cholera in the Crimean War.

One of the things I loved about Claire was her gentleness - it was so easy for me to love her and want to look after her. But that was also what the cancer liked and she had no meaningful resistance against that most devastating illness. As a Christian Scientist I was torn between hoping that medicine would find an answer and believing that the power of prayer and positive belief was all that was needed. But Claire was getting weaker and nothing seemed to make any difference. Although she did rally for a month or two after Jane's first birthday and we had some lovely days in the late spring and early summer.

One day in June, David Abell asked for a meeting with me. The business had continued to grow and prosper and was now in its third year as a PLC.

"Have you done any sums lately on the value of Ford and Slater?" he asked.

"I have other things on my mind right now David, as you might imagine," I replied.

"Of course, I'm sorry Bill; I didn't mean to be insensitive. I'll come straight to the point. We - Leyland that is - have been approached by Unilever; they want to buy out the truck division and that, of course, includes Ford and Slater. Would you consider selling your share?"

"What are we worth?" I asked.

David had the answers at his finger tips, "For a deal which would include share retention about eighteen pounds a share. More like sixteen if it were cash only."

"Probably then, but only for cash," was my reply, "...and only if I can stay on as MD."

This set in motion a maelstrom of behind the scenes activity that had to be hidden from public view. If any notion got out, to the workforce or to the market, all hell would break loose and an awful lot of damage could be done. Life for me and all the other directors would be a constant barrage of questions and criticism.

Meanwhile, Claire's condition was deteriorating. Talk about timing! I hoped we could get all the business sorted soon, so I could set about giving Claire and my two daughters all the attention they deserved. I was stretched to breaking point - in every direction it seemed. Looking back now, I wonder how I held it all together – but perhaps I didn't and everyone was too kind to say anything.

At last, everything was in place for the transfer of all the private shares in Ford and Slater - Tom's, Vic's, Ken's, Mother's and mine. We had all agreed and were selling at eighteen pounds a share - the transfer scheduled for August 16th 1973.

On the 15th August the front page headline of our regional evening newspaper, the Leicester Mercury, read: "Ford and Slater sold for £6.3 million to Unilever".

I bought a copy and took it home. I was to announce the takeover to the workforce the following morning.

Claire was lying in bed. The cancer, having spread, was now in her liver so she had been having morphine injections. I showed her the headline. She didn't open her eyes but asked me to read it to her. She attempted to sit up and listen as I read the article aloud. When I'd finished she slumped back on her pillows saying, "I'm so thrilled that this is the end of all those years of worrying."

I looked at the clock; it was seven in the evening and the sun shone golden through the bedroom window. That night she fell to sleep in my arms and I soon followed. Waking at about five the next morning, I showered and dressed and went to re-join Claire on the bed. Her breathing seemed erratic. I shook her gently, but she didn't wake. I talked to her, asking if she could hear me.

She nodded and murmured, "Hasn't God taken me yet?"

I opened the famous Methodist book – House of Prayer – which was on the bedside table and read from the opening lines: "When I awake in the arms of the Lord…"

She smiled and I lay down close beside her, beginning to

contemplate the day which lay ahead. Gradually I realised her breathing had changed, becoming shallower and less discernable. Between five to seven and seven o'clock I counted five breaths and then there were no more. Her spring of life had wound down and run out; she had passed away without me even realising it was about to happen.

If Father's dying had felt like a sledgehammer blow, this was like an asteroid colliding with the Earth from space. My mind was in turmoil with a million thoughts racing and crowding in my brain. One of my first thoughts, however, was one of relief that her suffering was over; she had been so incredibly brave right up to her last breath.

I was close friends with our doctor who only lived three miles away. I rang him and he came immediately. He was a legend in the area, his name being Philip Bell, who in later years was given the MBE for services to medicine. He wrote out the death certificate and gave me eight Valium tranquilisers which I took straightaway.

The previous day I had asked Claire's best friend, Richenda, who was also a Quaker, to collect our girls Kerry and Jane and it wasn't until a month later that she told me Claire had said goodbye that afternoon to her infant children.

I left the house as soon as I could to go to Ford & Slater where all fourteen managers were waiting in the board room. I confirmed that we had sold the business the night before to

Unilever. I apologised for the fact that I couldn't have told them any earlier but assured them that all their jobs were safe as Unilever wanted us to expand with UAC African interests.

Having done the unavoidable, I went to Richenda's house in Stoneygate to break the sad news. I asked her for a tumbler of brandy and to give me ten minutes before sending Kerry in to me. Jane was too young at sixteen months and I remembered how Claire had taught her to walk only three months earlier. When Kerry came in I took one look at her and told her that her mother had just passed away. She ran into my arms saying," Don't worry Daddy, we'll look after you."

Leaving Richenda's, I went home to Claire for the last time, driving the girls back to our house in Great Glen where Clare's mother and her sister Sonja had been staying for the past week.

Shortly afterwards the undertakers arrived and I helped them to carry her out of the house.

★   ★   ★

The Quaker Star

*""You do Bill, but you're not a Quaker and I don't know what will
become of us if you carry on working like you do."
We agreed to differ..."*

And I can listen to thee yet;
Can lie upon the plain
And listen, till I do beget
That golden time again.

O blessèd Bird! the earth we pace
Again appears to be
An unsubstantial, faery place;
That is fit home for Thee!

From the poem To the Cuckoo
by William Wordsworth

Chapter 15

The Cuckoo

As I write my memoirs I am re-living many parts of my life over again in my mind, more vividly than just recalling events, places and people. I see an old photograph and the emotion returns. A part of the hurt, the pride or the joy of those times envelopes me and I become immersed in my past to momentarily live those days again. But what I did in the days, weeks and months following Claire's death, other than just getting through somehow, I am not entirely sure. I had a lot of help, I know that, and I certainly found out who my real friends were; I was surprised by one or two on both sides of the help divide.

Outside help came in the shape of nannies, invaluable to me and my girls, as I wrestled with coming to terms with life after death and my new role as managing director of a PLC subsidiary of a mighty global corporation.

The primary motivation of that corporate giant, it seemed to me, was to grow as big and as fast as it could in every direction possible. There were flocks of executives on the lookout to target companies they could acquire. I also now had to answer on a daily basis to people I didn't know and had never met.

And, for the first time in my life, I had a price on my head. They took no time in telling me that the price was far too high, or more accurately, the salary package I had retained from my Ford and Slater days was about fifty percent higher than any equivalent executive in the Unilever group. When we took Ford and Slater public, I had not only organised a basic 12K salary but also a bonus of 1% of the pre-tax profits which, by the time we sold to Unilever, amounted to 22K per year in 1973 and it was this incentive bonus that caused the salary problem.

And the chairman forcefully pointed out at our group monthly meeting in London, "What is even more unacceptable is that there are two of you on the same package!"

We had refused to negotiate down as the growth at Ford and Slater had continued and it was our job to increase those profits, without which we would be back on 12K basic salary per year.

After a year Unilever's response was that Vic was to be made redundant, as his chairman's role at Ford and Slater was unnecessary with major policy decisions having to be made in London. Reluctantly, I accepted their decision but made it clear that it was London's responsibility to talk to Vic and not mine.

Vic was heading towards retirement anyway at the age of fifty eight and he was given a generous severance settlement, including a paid up pension. All this was on top of the money he would have received for the shares he sold on the takeover so he was now a very wealthy man. I never met him again after he was made redundant - he died of a heart attack in his sleep just six weeks after leaving the company. I attended his funeral and it was a very full church as he had made many friends. Tom Slater played the role of patriarch, albeit subtly, but I noticed.

I paid my respects and I was sad; he'd been with Ford and Slater since before the war; a brilliant salesman and customer relationship builder – a real people person, just not a Bill Ford person. He wasn't cremated and even if he had been I would have had no urge to follow through with my egg-timer threat. I've often wondered if it had been me who had died first, would he have danced on my grave? I still had a year or two to go before I turned forty and I wondered if his prediction that I would be dead before then might yet come true. But I'm glad we'd chosen to differ yet respect each other a long time before he died.

I was up and down to London so often after the takeover that I decided to buy a flat near our headquarters in Blackfriars so I could stay there Monday to Friday. The flat overlooked the river Thames and was only a fifteen minute walk from the offices. I drove down there, left the car in the underground car park at HQ, and walked to and from my flat each day.

As was my preference and still is, I would get to my desk early. At six am on a London weekday morning, the half-mile walk

245

to my office allowed me to reflect and to put myself and that small part of the great metropolis into perspective...

The littered streets, untidy with yesterday's detritus, have the air of a ghost town. Autumn leaves swirl among the wrappers and paper waste, ambling aimless as tumble weed but keeping me company until deflected by the draught from a passing bus or refuse lorry. Trains clatter at two or three minute intervals into and out of Blackfriars Station and over the bridge attesting to life going on somewhere in the capital, if not in this place, just yet. In London, the early morning seems easy with its physical emptiness, almost sighing with relief, yet imprinted with nostalgia's ghosts - like the feeling at a fairground the morning after the fair has packed up and gone - only the rubbish and flattened grass mark out the memory of the swarming crowds just hours before.

At Blackfriars Station, a smattering of people emerges as life begins to return. In an hour or so, on any weekday, waves of humanity will flow in every direction, bottle-necked at crossings, to be released just in time before the pressure of the crowd spews them into the path of hooting, fuming traffic. Almost impossible to imagine at that early hour, but those pavements take the footfall of a Division One football crowd every sixty minutes of every weekday morning rush hour...

I paid sixteen thousand pounds for my one bedroomed flat in

the autumn of 1977. I did a quick search on Google recently and the same flat in the same location is now on sale for over half a million pounds. The world's gone crazy!

I don't remember any names, or maybe I prefer not to say, but on one or two of my weekday nights I did find solace in the arms of a willing girl I had known only for hours. Or perhaps a lady from the office would keep me company, to hear my tales of flying through a monsoon or over Kilimanjaro and to listen as I describe the daffodils on the drive leading up to the Stone House.

Please excuse the hackneyed metaphors here but they do fit well in describing the rapid elevation of my career. For their pound of flesh - and because they knew I would work my socks off - I climbed the greasy corporate pole rapidly and within the first year of Ford & Slater becoming part of the Unilever group I was appointed as Managing Director of all the companies in the UK dealing with the automotive industry. And soon after this I was to take over the rest of Unilever's automotive operations world wide.

Coinciding with the takeover of Ford & Slater, Unilever had created a holding company called UAC International. You may recall the United Africa Company from my days in Africa; they were the parent company of Gailey & Roberts of 'Piss-pots to Pangas' fame. In the 1970s, as our colonies sought ever more separation from the UK, it was decreed that all companies trading in African countries had to have an operating company registered in the country of trading. Unilever created this new company, UAC International PLC, as a holding company to which all Unilever companies world wide must report. In this way they were able to satisfy the requirement of the African authorities and still retain control of their assets and trading positions. You may also recall from my early days in Africa, in that little office in Johannesburg in 1960, the shifting of bits of paper.

There is no statement that I have ever heard about corporate life that is truer than this one: If you give your life to the company they will take it!

By 1975, at the age of 36, I had become the youngest unit head out of all ten divisions of UAC International and had more than 11,000 employees under my control in more than 40 companies of which I was managing director. I could now over rule everyone I had ever dealt with in my African days and the thought still makes me smile to this day. However, that was not my modus operandi of how to run a business.

I did get involved with a number of take-overs in those early days as MD of the Motors Division and there's one I'd like to share that does give an example of how I dealt with a situation which was a buy out from the other side.

The company was called Autogem. They had built up a business since the early 1950s buying auto parts in bulk – exhausts, tyres, shock absorbers and the like - then splitting the packs and creating sales and distribution channels to sell the products individually to the larger market place. Unilever wanted in and had tried four times, unsuccessfully, to buy the company. I had done some research and knew the owners wanted to sell but were playing hard to get - probably to keep the price high. I'd arranged a meeting with the major shareholder and Unilever had said I could go up to three and three quarters of a million pounds to do the deal.

"I'll not sell for less than three and a half million, and that's final." This was as far as we'd got to as we left Autogem's offices to go for lunch at one o' clock. I knew we were going to a nearby restaurant and had fixed it for three of my co-directors to join me. I had asked my chairman in London to ring me in the afternoon and I'd primed him to play along with what ever I said to him on the phone.

"He'll not go below three and a half..." I spoke into the telephone clearly as I looked into the eyes of my adversary, shaking my head as I spoke.

"He'll not accept three and a quarter, for sure!" I was still looking into my opponents eyes and still shaking my head. My opponent shook his head too, in agreement with me. He was on my side now and I put down the phone. Back in Autogem's offices we agreed on a deal for Unilever to buy Autogem for three million four hundred thousand pounds. Including lunch it had taken me four and a half hours of negotiation to get that deal. My brief had been to get in, offer three and three quarters of a million and get out.

Back at the office the next day the conversation with my chairman went something like this:

"Why didn't you just offer him what we said and get out, instead of wasting all that time when you might have lost the deal?"

"I've saved at least a hundred and fifty thousand pounds on what I knew he would settle for. When was the last time you earned more than thirty thousand pounds an hour?"

Autogem became one of the most profitable parts of the motors division, making over a million pounds per annum – not a bad pay back period for £3.4 million.

Soon after I left in 1983, the corporate hand of governance job description and job values interfered; we had van salesman who made their money by being incentivised as a major part of their income and Unilever insisted that these were brought into line. We lost over 50% of our driver salesmen which directly impacted on profitability.

The logistics involved in managing my domestic situation had become ever more tiresome. The nannies I had the good fortune, or otherwise, to hire never seemed to last long; I was forever on the phone to the agency for a replacement. I felt pushed from pillar to post and so were Kerry and Jane. I often felt wretched on leaving them after a blissful weekend, but as I have said, the corporation will take all of your life if you let them and it felt like I couldn't stop them.

I was still running Ford and Slater, as well as the rest of the world, but I had mastered the art of delegation, just about, and the foundation company of my career was on a healthy course. I managed to spend two days a week, split between Ford and Slater and the other companies under my charge, at the offices in Leicester. Whether she found me or I found her I cannot say now after more than 40 years, but Judith came into my life and created a much longed for order for me and my girls. She was the personal assistant to Ford and Slater's Finance Director and was very good looking. There was nothing casual about our relationship once it started, but our first meeting was not like "Breakfast at Tiffany's" - full of anticipation and moonlight serenades. We literally bumped into each other in the office one day and she said something like, "Oh, hello Bill Ford, how are you today?"

The rest is history, an awful lot of history…

We dated, made friends with each other, and I introduced her to Kerry and Jane. She gave up her job at Ford and Slater to become their nanny. I married her and we had two children together, Ian and Julia. We lived in a sort of staccato harmony for a while, but all the time my business life was sapping away any long term happy union we could have had. By the time either of us realised what wasn't happening it was all too late…

*   *   *

No man is an island,

Entire of itself,

Every man is a piece of the continent,

A part of the main.

If a clod be washed away by the sea,

Europe is the less.

From the poem No Man is an Island

by John Donne

252

Chapter 16

Deserts, Mountains and Islands

In the compiling of this book I have had to make certain decisions about what to put in and what to leave out. A biography about a life lived as full as mine could run into many volumes, especially as my memory has retained and can recall so much detail. I realise and respect that my version of events may not be in accord with another's; after all, that immortal elegant phrase from Gustav Flaubert's Madame Bovary – 'There is no truth; There is only perception' - resounds in my head with every line written. With this at the forefront of my mind I have chosen not to tell the details of certain aspects of my personal life where those involved are still a part of my life and could be hurt by my perception of events. The public record is there for those who wish to explore further and I am content that my story, as you read it here, is a sincere and accurate account of the important and fundamental events that have shaped me into the person I have become. I am also acutely aware that too much detail would become boring for you and I would lose your interest.

There have been times when I have felt that I was all on my own, that I was an island; sometimes of my own volition and making, but often it was caused by circumstance. I was an island when Claire died, out of necessity on occasion and out of selfishness when I couldn't cope and needed to hide away for a while. Judith found me on this island and I welcomed her into my family, but I was swept away by the tornado of senior management in a global corporation. By 1980 I was travelling extensively on 3 continents and I was hardly ever at home – sometimes I wondered if I even knew where home was.

When Judith moved in with us we were still living in Great Glen, in the house that I had bought for Claire's final birthday only four months before she died. I guess Judith felt the ghost of Claire was too evident and in 1975 we moved to Rothley on The Ridgeway into a house called Tall Trees. This coincided with my first involvement with the Great Central Railway, the then redundant line, coincidentally running only four hundred yards from Tall Trees. But that tale will be told in the next part of the book, and as most of those I met and who will feature throughout my GCR days have broad shoulders the aforesaid omission of detail will be not be necessary!

It was pretty clear by 1982 that the sun was setting on the old British colonial world and, in Africa especially, independence was being declared state by state. UAC International was faced with a seventy four million pound deficit as Nigeria was going bankrupt and could not pay its bills. In two years, from 1980 to 1982, their currency, the Naira, went from one Naira to the pound to more than fifty to the pound making all imported products unaffordable. To give you an idea of the impossible situation there, the price of Bedford trucks rose from around five and a half thousand each, in fully knocked down state from the UK, to more than fifty thousand each. We then had to pay for transport and assembly in Lagos. With this written large on every wall it was time for me to leave and in March 1983 I gave Unilever three months notice.

With my long term colleague and very good friend ever after, Peter Regan, I embarked on a whirlwind tour of all of our suppliers – in America, Japan and Africa. In Detroit we visited the Henry Ford factory. We stayed in the best suite in the best hotel there, the Hotel Marriot. Booking in as Bill Ford and Mr Regan caused quite a stir upon our arrival and all eyes were upon us from the staff.

Leaving Detroit we flew first class to Boston. I had bought, as investment properties, four houses in a ski resort in Vermont and Peter and I were to visit there for a long weekend on our way back to the UK. The service on the plane was typical of American Airlines in the eighties - poor - and the hostess was a very brash American bordering on the outright rude. Peter had a particularly wicked sense of sarcastic humour and with his best English public school accent he was doing his utmost to annoy the attendant. The pilot had just announced the beginning of our descent into Logan airport when Peter ordered a bottle of champagne with a bucket of ice. He had taunted our hostess during the two hour flight saying, "Do you know who we are? This is my very good friend Bill FORD and I am Mr REGAN and I would urge you to pay us both the utmost respect."

(The Chairman of Ford Motors was also called Bill, by the way.) She got so wound up about it that she went to check on the boarding manifest to verify what he'd said.

First class on board those narrow bodied jets had space for just ten passengers, so everyone in first class shared in the conversations. Peter and I had been discussing what culinary delights we might enjoy that evening in our hotel. Boston is a world renowned fishing port, especially noted for the finest sea creatures of the decapod crustacean genus, so we decided that a crab salad would be in order. On the final descent, just as the pilot lifted the nose of the plane and dropped the power in preparation for reversing the engines upon landing - when all goes quiet for a few moments - Peter blurted out, "I hear you can get crabs in Boston!"

Sharing first class with us was a big tall Texan, complete with his ten gallon hat. He retorted in his Southern states drawl, "You certainly can if you ain't too careful!"

The whole cabin erupted with laughter, including our brash Yankee air hostess.

Peter Regan took over from me as head of motors division at

UAC, but soon after that Unilever closed down all of its UAC divisions. They sold off most of the assets, causing huge grief to the families who had sold to them in good faith; they'd been made the same promises as I had made to our people at Ford and Slater. Ford and Slater was sold on to Abdul Latif Jamil of Toyota fame, who were expanding in Britain, as well as Hartwells and Hartford in Oxford. Ford & Slater continue to this day under new management, still thriving as the leading distributors for DAF who bought the assets off Leyland Motors. It was a great shame that Leyland closed as the government of the day refused to invest. This included BMC. The Government of France supported Renault who were in the same position as Leyland and the Dutch government came to the aid of DAF at that time too. Both Renault and DAF now thrive. It is almost inconceivable to realise that the Leyland 600 engine was sold to DAF and that the turbo charged derivatives of that have been developed by DAF into one of the best engines in the industry.

But others were not so lucky, disappearing completely after having been absorbed and their assets liquidated, leaving no trace of the original company at all. I know that when all is boiled down, business is just about money and when a business is sold for an agreed amount that ought to be the end of it - the seller should just walk away and enjoy the proceeds. But if you give your life to something, a part of you will stay with it; our own history is intertwined with the experience and our footprints remain there.

Even in a minor way, I bet there's a metal desk somewhere in Africa, the one I first sat at in Johannesburg as a lowly service parts clerk; there will be a dent and a scratch on it from when I moved the furniture around to get a better view of a couple of girls I had taken a shine to in the office! Their names were Jackie von Staden and Hettie Pretorius but I didn't meet them again after I left. Both of these girls were lovely and, being Afrikaans, prove my non-racial aspect towards life.

When I reached Nairobi and Dar Es Salaam, after going on safari with Quentin More and his stepson, I came back to 35 airmail letters from various girlfriends in South Africa. The trouble was, they all wanted to come and visit so I decided to go AWOL.

The cull that took place in those final days of UAC International was dreadful indeed. I was involved at the beginning of the onslaught. There were confidential memos sent to all senior managers that stated you couldn't sack any one on a Friday for fear of them hanging themselves over the weekend. Private security men would accompany managers and previous owners off the premises to make sure nothing was taken away that could be used against the company. Often they were marched off the site of a company which they'd fought to build over decades. Within a few short months all traces of any UAC International PLC financial involvement had disappeared, almost as if they'd never existed. On my last evening, the chairman of UAC International took me out to the Savoy for dinner. He said to me that I had done the right thing in choosing to leave and that he feared for all senior managers within the group. Within 24 months even the head office had closed and been sold. The commissions that UAC relied on to function disappeared almost overnight and all operations run by them were transferred to the relevant country concerned in Africa. The initial effect was that I lost a third of my London head office UAC staff and as unit head it fell to me to make each of them redundant. I decided that I was much better at growing companies than watching their demise, so in March 1983 I handed in my three months notice.

And so, in the summer of '83, in the forty-sixth year of my life, I found myself unemployed. The thought did cross my mind that I could afford never to work again. I was a millionaire a few times over, unencumbered by any trust fund whose rules I'd have to bow and scrape to, but it didn't feel very comfortable at all. For me, money - the acquisition of it or the possession of it - was never an end in itself; money is to live with and have fun with. The more you have the better you can live and the more fun you can have - but it is not the be all and end all of anything. I know this might sound flippant and blasé to those of you who haven't had my opportunities, but apart from the glitter, the better table at a restaurant and perhaps a faster mode of transport, it is still other values in life which make you really happy. The love and appreciation from those close to you and those you are responsible for is the holy grail of happiness. Chasing money never made any one happy. When you get it, you find queues of people wanting to take it off you. The world is full to bursting with self-centred folk over-eager to fleece an approachable and generous man in the pursuit of their own agenda. The knocker on my door has worn very thin over time...

Home life with my newly expanded family seemed somewhat tame after the cut and thrust of UAC, but we enjoyed a holiday or two during my redundant summer.

I had filled in the necessary forms to sign out as a non resident of the UK and, after several months in Vermont with our marriage in a perilous state, I tried to develop my business in the US whilst Judith and family stayed in the UK back in Rothley.

I was chairman of Leyland's Blue Line Distributors Association and a head hunter in Oxford asked me to help with recruiting suitable candidates for overseas positions.

I arrived at his offices in Oxford and after a short chat by way of introduction, he left me for a while as he was in another meeting. He'd handed me a job specification brief asking if I knew anyone who could fulfil the role. The salary on offer was a hundred thousand a year and the job was perfect for someone like me. It was to head up the Toyota franchise in Saudi Arabia, the second largest in the world selling 160,000 vehicles a year. I had dealt with the Saudis before and found them to be honourable businessmen once you had gained their trust. When my contact came out from his meeting ready to go for lunch he asked me if I could think of anyone. My reply was, "What's the rate of income tax in Saudi Arabia?"

He answered, "Nought, zero percent."

"You'd better interview me then," said I.

Shortlisted at first, I became one of the final two to be considered. We both had to fly out to Jeddah to be interviewed by the Jamil family. I was selected and six weeks later was on my way back to Saudi to take up my position as General Manager of the ALJ franchise.

Pound for pound I worked harder in Saudi than I ever had before or have since - and I earned a sight more too. But I loved every minute of the challenge. The Jamil family were very wealthy and part of the biggest business group in that nation.

I didn't see much of my own family whilst I was out there, although they did come over for every school holiday after I had been there for about four months. Laws were strict and freedoms for ordinary folk were very restricted; but ex-pats at senior level lived in luxurious compounds and most of our own ways of life were maintained - as long as they were contained in there. I was invited to the homes of my employers and was amazed to witness the overt luxury they enjoyed. My initial reaction was that it was hypocrisy for them to live in such opulent splendour while allowing ordinary folk to live in starkly opposite restricted suppression. But, as I got to know how things worked there, I began to understand that it was an ancient feudal culture thrust into the riches of the twentieth century on tidal waves of petro-carbon. This had changed the balance of their society with only a few decades in which to come to terms with it - it was inevitable and a natural progression of sociological evolution. Had oil been as valuable in the days when our empire was on the ascendant, Saudi Arabia would have been another jewel in Queen Victoria's crown. But they'd had to find their own way of dealing with it. The pecking order had no doubt assembled along the lines of the survival and success of the smartest, biggest and most ruthless - as indeed our own feudal system had evolved centuries before. Then, when order had been beaten in to the masses and they were controlled by the wrath of God through religious extremism, those in possession of the wealth protected themselves with laws and Fort Knox style palaces.

Mohammed Jamil was a lovely man and was the partner I reported to with the older brother Yousef as president. In the Jamil palace every courtesy was afforded to their guest - which is what we as employees were and we were never allowed to forget it. If you can live with that hypocrisy and manage on the massive wages they allocate, you can become pretty well off, especially when you take the zero tax rate into consideration.

After eighteen months however, in the autumn of 1985, in spite of me coming to terms with that way of life and beginning to enjoy the challenges and to succeed, the Jamil brothers fell out with each other and all senior English personnel were let go.

For the second time in my life I was out of work, but two hundred thousand pounds the richer and foot loose and fancy free. So Judith, my growing children and I, took an extended vacation in America based in Vermont, in the January of 1986. I was continuing to run my little nest of businesses and was in daily contact with those back in the UK who were running things. Towards the end of our holiday I received a call via my secretary to ask if I could return to the UK and meet with Sheik Abdullah al Kraidees – the president of Al Jazirah, which was owned by the second son of the then Crown Prince M'ttab. All I knew from the phone call was that he wished to meet me and discuss an opportunity that had arisen that might interest me. The request was for me to meet him the next morning in London. I could not do this as I was 160 miles north of Boston, but I could catch the 9pm flight on the following day, I knew the flight times from Boston well and worked out my plan to meet Abdullah al Kraidees at 9am the day after tomorrow.

Leaving my family to stay on for a few more days, I arrived at London Heathrow at 5 am. I took a taxi into central London and had a good breakfast at a restaurant near to London Bridge that I used to visit often in my days with UAC.

Sheik Abdullah, dressed in a business suit and with a perfect English accent, told me of the opportunity. He, together with other Royal Princes, had been offered the first Ford of America franchise in Saudi Arabia for thirty years. Until now American companies had been forbidden to trade in Arabic countries - the Israeli dilemma, on all sides of the argument, having made all communication difficult. But a new regime of accord, together with the growing commercialisation of Arab nations with their oil reserves, made it impossible to ignore. I told Sheik Abdullah that I was indeed interested and felt that my time in his country was not yet over and I that I had still much more to give.

He said I was to go out on my own initiative and meet with the two princes heading up the project: Princes Mittab and Turki. Sheik Abdullah would provide the introductions necessary to get an audience and he himself was to head up the new Ford enterprise.

Again, I was treated as a guest and every courtesy was shown to me. The most important thing I was asked was this: "We will not be able to afford those generous terms you enjoyed with the Toyota franchise as this is a "Green Field" opportunity and none of us know how it will all transpire. That being the case, why would you want to return to Saudi Arabia?"

I said that I was keen to return because I found that doing business in Saudi was much more pleasurable and satisfying than it was in Europe; the challenge of a "Green Field" opportunity excited my ambitions and fitted well with my experiences throughout my career.

I was offered a two year contract, eventually, on a pay scale that was in fact more generous that the Toyota one. Living accommodation was upgraded and my family were allowed to join me; although they decided to stay in Rothley and come out for every holiday.

The pressure of work was extreme and I began to suffer from stress. I got shingles followed by a particularly nasty urinary tract infection. But, I still managed to get to work each day for 6.30 am.

Saudi Arabia, supposedly having Thursday afternoon and Friday off as their weekend, and Ford U.S. having Saturday and Sunday off as theirs, made things difficult. To make matters worse Saudi Arabia was 9 hours ahead, which entailed staying in the office throughout the evening for long talks with Detroit. This meant leaving the office at 10pm after the dining rooms had closed, but the coffee shop was still open, enabling me to get to bed at 11.

Dealing with eleven Saudi directors and me having no ability to speak Arabic was not easy, especially when the senior management – the Princes and Abdullah – would usually take a week to make an appointment. But even so, at the end of year one we turned a profit, increasing that considerably at the end of year two. Everyone hailed it a signal success and on a recent Google search I found that the Al Jazirah Ford franchise, in March 2017, had opened the largest dealer showroom in the world in Riyadh.

Having fulfilled my two year contract, I asked to leave at the end of 1989. My resignation was turned down flat. I needed to return home, my health was suffering and I was becoming paranoid with the difference in culture. My Saudi bosses would often play tricks on foreign employees, calling them into disciplinary meetings on a whim just to see them get nervous about what measures might come into force if they were found to be at fault. I had got it into my head that if I didn't toe their line on some matter or other it could easily be arranged to have drugs placed in my car - then I would be in court facing the death penalty if found guilty. I had seen cases where a foreigner had been found guilty and taken all the way to have the sentence carried out – which in their culture is beheading – only to be reprieved at the last minute. All this to teach a foreigner who wouldn't toe the line a lesson, so rumour had it...

I recalled the dark curse that Miss Knight had put upon me as I'd left Stoneygate College at the age of seven; about me ending up swinging on the end of a rope. That now seemed tame compared to a gruesome end such as this. No, Saudi Arabia was no place to fall foul of the authorities; I was an Englishman and I wanted to return home. After the third time of asking to leave they finally agreed and I thankfully spent the Christmas of 1989 back in Leicestershire.

Home wasn't so easy to define, however. I had earned a good deal of tax free income since the beginning of 1984, more than five years ago now. If I returned home as a UK resident I would owe hundreds of thousands of pounds in tax at UK rates - as if I had lived and worked in Britain all those years. That didn't seem right at all as I had not had the benefits of living and working there, so I looked for options. I considered the Channel Islands, but turned this down because property was extortionately priced for those not born there. I had property in the US and I tried to buy the business which had developed at the ski resort nearby. The holding business – Hawk Mountain Corporation - had entered into bankruptcy administration. I had sufficient collateral to buy the assets and then I could set about developing the resort as a going concern. I spent six months trying to understand the US legal and banking systems before I realised the project was not for me. In America, when buying a business's assets that are in administration, you commit to taking on all the previous debts as well. But they don't tell you that until the eleventh hour.

The reason that Hawk Mountain went bust was that they had seriously miscalculated the costs of running the operation. For six months of the year the temperatures are around zero and below, falling to minus thirty in mid winter, and the fuel costs are enormous. Doing business in the USA is steeped in complicated laws and the banking system and laws change from state to state. I found I needed a lawyer every step of the way, even for the smallest business transaction, and they don't come cheap at all. In the UK you can put a bid in for the assets of a bankrupt company to the liquidator, who is an independent, professionally qualified accountant; you and he can agree on a deal and complete simply with ordinary contracts and exchange of money. Over there you have to deal with banks, lawyers, administrators, courts, creditors and public servants. In all I lost about a million dollars in six months and had nothing to show for it except the experience to know that the United States is no place for the likes of me.

My marriage to Judith being over, it was time to end it properly and finally. Having decided to settle in the Isle of Man, I bought a total of about twenty flats and houses as an investment and set up a small finance company with the remit to help small businesses. The tax system allowed for me to retain my earned income from Saudi together with the money from Ford and Slater without penalty.

The investment in the flats in Douglas and my small finance

company was a good start. I appointed a solicitor who worked and lived on the island who was able to act for both Judith and myself in our divorce. This would not normally be possible in England due to the obvious conflict of interest. It allowed for non-contentious proceedings, cutting down on the costs for both sides and providing for a better financial arrangement all round. Judith received the house – by this time one in nearby Quorn - and a generous allowance for herself until she remarried. I made provision for all of our children, for their upkeep and their schooling at private schools.

I had parted from Judith on five separate occasions and whilst we could not live together we remain friends to this day. I was sad that it hadn't worked out and not just because I was poorer for it after the settlement. After Claire had died I really don't know what would have become of me, Kerry and Jane without Judith. She saved me and held us together in the best way that she could. We never really wholly loved each other, but convenience proved to be a powerful bond.

The break up did have a detrimental effect on our own two children, Ian and Julia. They were at that critical early adolescent age and I have no doubt that the break up of our marriage hurt them terribly. Julia became anorexic to the degree that she became so ill that, had she lost another two pounds in weight, she would have been hospitalised and may not have ever recovered. She came to live with me in Douglas and after several months of careful attention she improved. I had set targets, the grand prize being two weeks with me in one of the best hotels in Disney World, Florida. She had been there as a four year old and had loved it.

She had been living with me on the island for nine months when I dropped her off to stay at her mother's after the Disney holiday and I continued on to the Isle of Man. On the Sunday night Judith rang me at seven in the evening to say that Julia now wanted to live in England with her. I went absolutely berserk and suddenly got a terrible headache which developed into the worst pain I have ever had. A violent period of sickness and diarrhoea overcame me. It was so bad that I called an ambulance and then rang Judith, asking her to check on me in the morning as I feared for my life. She laughed and accused me of faking it to get Julia back. With that the ambulance arrived and took me to the hospital which was a mile and half away. They gave me a pethidine injection, asked me a lot of questions and then discharged me, leaving me to walk back home, saying that I was suffering from food poisoning. By five in the morning I was again in great pain and when my secretary came in I asked her to ring the doctor. Three days later I was back in hospital and after another two days of tests I was air-freighted to the mainland by air ambulance, to Walton Hospital near Liverpool for scans, as it was thought I had a brain tumour. Of course I tried with all my Christian Science faith to overcome this with the power of positive prayer, but I really did think I was going to die. More to the point, there were times when I wished I would, just to get rid of the constant intense pain. After many tests over several days I was visited by the senior consultant.

"Well Mr Ford, it seems you are one of the lucky ones. You have suffered a subarachnoid brain haemorrhage - an aneurism of a blood vessel in your brain. Less than ten percent of those who have suffered this survive. There is no surgery necessary as it has healed itself, but you will need to rest for a few months to prevent a re-occurrence. We'll send you back to the hospital on the Isle of Man for them to keep an eye on you for a few days and then you can go home."

He shook my hand and carried on with his rounds leaving me wondering if maybe my guardian angel was still looking out for me.

It took me a year to recover from the brain haemorrhage. I would lose concentration easily and all I could do was go for a walk. I did enjoy this aspect of the island as there is some amazing scenery and landscape to discover. It was and still is the perfect place to retire; like Bournemouth but for those born north of Watford and west of Leicester. I pretended I'd retired when I left Unilever in the summer of 1983, then again after all senior management had been let go for the first time from Saudi, and yet again when I left the employ of Sheik Abdullah Al Kraidees in 1990. But this last retirement was for real and I hated it. I found that there is only so much one can do with free time; time that no one pays you for or time that is not spent on anything worthwhile. I couldn't spend much time in the UK for tax reasons and I couldn't do business there either for the same reasons.

With only a population of around seventy five thousand, The Isle of Man presented me with very little in the way of business opportunities. I was offered the Toyota franchise, an opportunity which equated to something along the lines of a car dealership in a small town. But with half the population being millionaires I calculated that selling Toyotas would not be profitable – Rolls Royces, Aston Martins or helicopters maybe, but not Toyotas – and Toyota was the only opportunity that was available.

There was one enjoyable annual distraction. The Island goes crazy every year at the end of May with the world famous TT races. It really is the Monaco Grand Prix on two wheels (some races on three wheels with sidecar events) but without the heat, the continental accents or the safety barriers. It is a wonder there aren't more deaths during race weeks. Watching from close up the speed they approach corners and the angles they achieve round bends is breathtaking. How they stay on the road is testament to their skill, bravery and downright suicidal stupidity. But other than these petrol fume filled days I was mostly bored and restless.

I am a man who needs company and I need someone to share

my life with. I did a lot of searching for a soul mate in the nineties but all to no avail. Worse than no avail - I got bewitched by a very attractive lady in 1997. It makes me wince to recall this disastrous episode in my life, but it does serve to demonstrate and emphasise the total waste of time the Isle of Man part of my life really was. We wined and dined in the priciest places the island had to offer and after a year, when we had been round them all, we got married in Mauritius, in the grounds of the most splendid hotel to be found in that idyllic paradise.

On reflection, it is clear that the only attraction she found in me was my money. On our wedding night she made some requests which stunned me, even as besotted and stupid as I was then. She asked if I would look after her even if I was gone and would I sign the house into her name.

You would think that I would have learned by then wouldn't you? At least Cruella (I dare not mention her real name for fear of the subarachnoid aneurism's return) hadn't pleaded pregnancy to ensnare me! But she was just as unfaithful and in the end even more avaricious than Maivis had proved to be. After two years of wining and dining my pants off I was diagnosed with an aggressive form of prostate cancer and Cruella upped sticks and left.

I had signed over the house in order to keep a sort of status quo, but I had used a clever lawyer to word the nuptial agreement that ring fenced any other assets if our marriage dissolved or upon my demise. This proved to be my saving grace. Within a week of my diagnosis and subsequent admission for treatment at Clatterbridge Cancer Centre in the Wirral, Cruella filed for divorce with an affidavit demanding at least half of all my worth and the house which I had put in her name which was valued at six hundred thousand. My worth of course was two million lighter after the settlement with Judith, but I still had assets worth a lot more than the house Cruella had made me sign over. In the end she settled out of court for less than the value of the house, because she was desperate for cash and I had only given her the right to live in the house and not to its value. At least I got that bit right.

My treatment was paid for by BUPA and after a year or so travelling back and forth, I was released from their care as the cancer had responded well to the treatment. I have to return twice a year to the Wirral for tests and attend my local doctor's surgery once a month for a blood test.

It was in the BUPA hospital on the Wirral, with treatment at nearby Clatterbridge, that I first met Debbie. She has been my saviour, my best friend, my companion and so much more than I could ever have deserved.

★   ★   ★

They pay very well but they make you earn every penny!
Sheik Abdullah al Kraidees – the president of Al Jazirah shakes hands
on the deal...

"So there are none I have found that I could say, 'Without this guy there'd be no railway today', except Lord Lanesborough."

Part Four

The (Nearly) Great Central
Railway 1973 – 2017

And I wonder,

Has the world forgotten the unseen

And ordinary heroes of today?

Has the world turned a blind eye

To the men and women who

Fight the everyday battles

To keep a child's hopes and dreams alive?

From the poem The Forgotten Heroes

by Nicole Gravell Pelegrino

Chapter 17

Forgotten Heroes

In more than forty years of being involved with The Great Central Railway I have met and worked with hundreds of fine men, women and children (of all ages!) who could be classed as heroes and yet, superficially, it seems unfair to single any one of them out.

It's often the leaders who are elevated on pedestals with statues made in their honour after they are gone. Others might have a plaque or a painting donated in gratitude, but for the majority there's only a memory, at most, which remains with the living and will die with them.

Those who have led "our" great railway have mostly been men with money and from the outside it could look as if they've bought their way into the leader's position. That is true to some extent, especially on the board of the GCR – past and present. It's the way of our world that this is so often the case and as long as the ability to lead and manage comes with the money, then progress and success usually follow. But along the meandering path of the history of the GCR we've had a mixed array of money with and without ability. In my time as leader I can honestly say that it's been the toughest test of my entire career and of all my abilities, to hold it all together. I've had to use brinkmanship, undue influence, financial inducements and plain downright belligerence at times to force a path out of disaster on many occasions - and I have lost friends along the way in so doing. But, as I have judged situations, it has been for the greater good as it often meant we could likely lose the railway if we didn't take drastic action; at times within hours from bankruptcy after the bank had pulled the plug. There were occasions when the "leaders" of the GCR had to run around a day before pay day asking managers, staff and volunteers to loan money to the company so they could pay the wages of employees and bills of suppliers.

In 2002, immediately after the death of my good friend and former president of the GCR David Clarke, there was a huge crisis as David had personally guaranteed the overdraught. The bank froze the account, left the railway floundering and I was asked to help, which I did, along with several others including Richard Lovatt and Graham Oliver; we got the bank back on side and were able to continue. After that time, it was clear to me that the railway could not possibly continue in its present structure. David, with others including me, had capitalised the railway since 1976 when we had both come on board together to help. Money bequeathed by David and donated by countless other benefactors great and small, was being held in the accounts of the group of "Friends of the Great Central", at that time called "The Main Line Steam Trust" (MLST) and there seemed to be inadequate co-operation between them and the operating company, causing the operating company to frequently run dry of funds. The money bequeathed and donated over the years was being ring-fenced unfairly for pet projects that weren't for the good of the whole railway. A ridiculous state of affairs in that the MLST had more than four hundred thousand pounds in its account and there was no majority among its ranks willing to see any transferred to help the operating company, which was going cap in hand every month to pay wages and repair infrastructure and rolling stock. Whilst David was alive things ran reasonably well; he could divert funds as and when needed because it had been largely his own money in the kitty and no one was going to act against him. In order to release those funds after David had died, I became president and from that position persuaded the board and the members of MLST to form "The David Clarke Railway Trust" with myself as chairman and Malcolm Freckelton as secretary. I know that this single act saved the railway and lost me many friends. But it streamlined the process of decision making and funding and slowly but surely the railway began on a path to sustainability. But I was still a resident of the Isle of Man and from there I was finding it difficult to get involved on a day to day basis. Although the railway was moving forward, I could clearly see that without an able captain at the helm the PLC would lurch from crisis to crisis. So in 2007 I gave up my legitimate tax efficient status, which over the years I calculate has cost me in excess of half a million pounds, and came back to run things properly. From then on, until I was forcibly retired in July of 2016, I worked seven days a week to create and manage teams that would ensure the future for years to come. As you will have read, throughout my career I have relied on team work to achieve success. I put the right people in the right roles, give them "wings" and then let them fly. Everyone I ever appointed I instilled with faith and confidence and then let them get on with the work. (I have even done this with Steve Johns, the co-writer of this book, and again I know I was right in my decision.) But I have always been there to help whenever needed.

I would offer this word of advice to the present leaders at the helm: Get involved in every aspect of the railway, with every single individual at what ever level he or she may be at; be seen and heard but you will have to earn their trust. Go and have a cup of tea with them personally. Don't just pay them lip service, they will mark you down as a fraud and not trust you; then they'll not give what you need to succeed, no matter how much money you pump in. And, most of all, do not delegate this most important of all tasks to anyone else.

Money alone will not create success. Passion alone will not create success. Management alone will also fail to deliver. You have to get involved from the bottom up; you have to strive to create that vital element of rapport, so that all parts of the enterprise feel honoured and respected. Do this and you will surely succeed. That's what I did throughout my career and especially at the Great Central, and that's what David Clarke did. That's also what a long forgotten hero by the name of Lord Lanesborough did, too.

And this is where this chapter will now dwell.

The presidents, directors and managers Lovatt, Clarke, Willet, me, Patching, Freckleton, Baines, Gough and Gregory et al could never have had a look in if it were not for this man and his family. I was in a meeting with him in the late 1970s and I was in awe of his easy authoritative manner with people. I noticed he always had a ready smile. We had a chat after the meeting and he asked me what school I had attended.

"Stowe – nineteen fifty to fifty five," I replied.

"I thought so…" the lord exclaimed.

"What school did you go to?" I enquired dimly.

"Stowe, you bloody fool!"

He then shook my hand firmly and we became good friends for the rest of his life.

Denis Anthony Brian Butler was born on the 28th October 1918 and became the 9th Earl of Lanesborough upon the death of his father, the 8th Earl, in 1950. Death duties had forced him to sell most of the 3,000 acres of his ancestral estate upon which Swithland Hall stood. He also inherited the titles of 10th Viscount Lanesborough and 12th Baron Newton-Butler. He was never allowed to sit in the House of Lords as he was an Irish peer and they had been barred from that privilege when Ireland had formally separated from the United Kingdom in 1922.

After he died aged eighty in 1998, I kept in touch with his widow Julia. I visited her often to update her on the railway and its people and we did become good friends. She was vital in the building of the Mountsorrel Branch which sadly she never saw completed. Without her permission it could never have even started. She died in 2015 at the age of 83 and in her will she left fifty thousand pounds to the railway together with her husband's scrapbook and photo album. Looking through them I was amazed at the level of his involvement, effort and the length of time he had strived to save the railway. There's a collage of a small sample of newspaper cuttings from his scrapbook in the photograph section - photo number 44.

He had started his campaign to save and preserve the line at about the same time as Ernest Marples asked Richard Beeching to become a member of an advisory group looking into the financial state of British Transport. Rivalry between the various lines and regions then present on British Railways meant that services on the GCR were being run down from the late fifties and Lord Lanesborough began forming action groups to bring it to the public's notice and to prevent further reductions in services.

Looking through the scrapbooks of his life I have formed the opinion that all of his adult life, apart from the second world war years where he was a major in the Leicester Yeomanry Regiment, seemed to be spent on serving his community at all levels. Although, from the photos, a lot of that service looked like presenting awards, often with a beautiful leading lady such as Yvonne de Carlo, a Miss World or others from the realm of theatre or cinema by his side.

He was friends with Princess Alexandra, Anthony Armstrong Jones, The Duke of Rutland, bishops, duchesses, members of parliament, leaders of nations and influential business men from all over the world. He was president of the Royal Society of Guide Dogs for the Blind, a director of the Cooperative society, a fully paid up member of ASLEF and a Justice of the Peace; he served on the Trent Regional Health Authority and became its vice chairman for four years from 1978. He was a member of the National Gas Consumers Council for five years from 1973.

His first wife was the daughter of Sir William Lindsay Everard of Leicestershire brewery fame, but that marriage ended in 1950 shortly after he took up his peerage. They had two daughters but the first died when she was only three years old in 1947. His second wife, Patricia Julia, had been his long time secretary and companion, and they eventually married in 1995.

But his greatest passion was for railways. He had built a six hundred feet long 00 gauge model railway in Swithland Hall which was a replica of the line from Carlisle to Fort William, presumably with tunnels, loops and fiddle yards to create the illusion of distance. It would be so easy for any one of us to dismiss all of Lord Lanesborough's service as merely paying lip service to the common man, whilst enjoying all the fruits that privilege, status and wealth can bestow; but I know better than that. I have worked alongside him when he would wield a broom or a spanner with equal aplomb. Often he would don a pair of overalls and get down and shovel the ash into a barrow, fill up an oil can for a driver, or serve a cup of tea to a volunteer. The GCR's first employee, Alen Grice, who was shed foreman fitter at Annesley right up to the end of steam and beyond, has often told me tales of his 'first apprentice' Lord Lanesborough. I have to admit that both were capable of colourful language in the appropriate setting and context in order to get things done! From different sides of the class divide it is interesting to muse upon the common language that we all understand and obey when it is needed.

In the nineteenth century Lord Lanesborough's grandfather smoothed the way, part-funding with land and money, for two very significant improvements in our little part of Merrie England. One was the creation of Swithland reservoir, completed in 1896, without which the rapidly growing city of Leicester would have faced crippling water shortages; the second is the building of the Great Central Railway across that reservoir and over part of the Lanesborough land, completed in 1899. I admit that both could be seen as a quid pro quo, what with the family's financial involvement in local quarrying, but history records no protest, only support, backing and positive influence. Without these advancements to our local civilisation we would all be the poorer. There is a rumour, which I haven't yet substantiated, that the Victorian Lord Butler negotiated the building of a small halt at Swithland for his own personal use, but that's perhaps a project for Steve Johns to take on for a contribution to MainLine magazine at some future date.

Moving on to the 9th Earl, my good friend Denis Butler, his influence in our story is much more direct. The newspaper cuttings in his scrapbooks tell of his battle to save the GCR in the early sixties, fighting the minister of transport at every turn, getting support from councils and politicians to forward realistic bids to buy out the line and at times he had meetings with Beeching and Marples in person. All his efforts only delayed the inevitable, but that delay was crucial in allowing time for people to gather and form the fledgling preservation movement; the offspring of which we now enjoy as our region's premier tourist attraction. If you think I am exaggerating as to how important all that delay was, just look how fast they ripped up the rest of the GCR from the mid-sixties. Lord Lanesborough fought tirelessly at every stage and was present in all the dealings to wrestle for the land, permission, fundraising and financing in our heritage railway's formative years.

I have entitled this chapter Forgotten Heroes; it could just as easily have been called Unsung Heroes but I think Forgotten fits best. The Unsung are all of those I mentioned earlier in this chapter – who have to sing for themselves perhaps?

It is to my shame, and should be to others who have shared this journey of the GCR with me, that we have not remembered Lord Lanesborough at all in any way that I can see.

There are certainly a number of contenders who might, on the surface, fit the role as our premier hero, but look a little closer and you'll find that they all got involved after it had been saved, including me! So there are none I have found that I could say, "Without this guy there'd be no railway today" except Lord Lanesborough. Take him out of our GCR history and all that we enjoy today would indeed be confined to history.

I look through book after book, read story after story, magazine after magazine and I find little mention of him at all. The latest excellent and most comprehensive tome on the GCR, the one on sale in Loughborough Station shop by Robin Jones, mentions him only twice and gives him little credit except as quoted in these two short pieces on pages 33 and 47 respectively:

Page 33 extract:

"A letter from Denis Anthony Brian Butler, the 9th Earl of Lanesborough, published in the Daily Telegraph on September 28th, 1965 read '...surely the prize for idiotic policy must go to the destruction of the, until recently, most profitable railway per ton of freight and per passenger carried in the whole British Railway system, as shown by their own operating statistics.

"These figures were presented to monthly management meetings until the 1950s, when they were suppressed as 'unnecessary' but one suspects really 'inconvenient' for those proposing Beeching-type policies of unnecessarily severe contractions of services...

"The railway is, of course, The Great Central, forming a direct continental loading gauge route from Sheffield and the north to the Thames Valley and London for Dover and France."

Page 47 extract:

"Local Landowner Lord Lanesborough, through whose estate the railway ran, became president of the group (Main Line Preservation Group) which embarked on a series of exhibitions and film shows to publicise its aims."

There are a couple of fuzzy photos in Robin Jones's book with Lord Lanesborough in them, but he doesn't warrant a mention on any caption. An irony that shouts out at me is that Beeching, the devil in our story, gets more page space than our real hero, the 9th Earl of Lanesborough!

So, in the hope that someone of influence today might read this, I'd like to make a suggestion:

In this year, 2018, which is the centenary of his birth, could we find a fitting way to commemorate Lord Lanesborough with the naming of an engine or one of our new projects - the bridge, the downsized museum - or perhaps the junction onto the Mountsorrel branch? Without permission from Countess Lanesborough the Mountsorrel branch could not have been rebuilt - it could be named Lanesborough Junction. It seems shameful that he is almost forgotten and remembered only in a few lines in a soft cover book...

Death duties having taken their final toll on the Earl after his mother died, he had to sell Swithland Hall and his beloved model railway (much of the model railway was sold to David Clarke, I believe) and he moved to Kegworth Lodge in the late 1970s, a far more modest home. He did ask me if I was interested in buying Swithland Hall. The asking price in 1980 was twenty five thousand pounds. I asked an architect to have a look around and he reported back to me that it would cost a fortune to restore and maintain, so I had no option but to decline the offer.

Having retired from public life, Lord Lanesborough spent his final decade as a gentleman of his own manor in a large house of stately proportions near Kelso, in Scotland. He died two days after Christmas in 1998 and, as he had no male heir, all the titles died with him. There remain just two references to his name: a little house in Swithland named Lanesborough Cottage and the five hundred to two and a half thousand pounds a night Lanesborough Hotel, off Hyde Park Corner in London. On the site of St George's Hospital, it is based on the old family home, sold in 1733, of the first Irish Viscount Lanesborough.

★   ★   ★

The GCR's first employee, Alen Grice

Drive on! Let all your fiery soul,
Your puissant heart that scorns control,
Your burnished limbs of circling steel,
The throb, the pulse of driving wheel...

From the poem
"To a Great Western Broad Gauge Engine and its Stoker"
by Horatio Brown

Chapter 18

Rich Boys' Toys

In the 1970's, when I first became involved with the Great Central Railway, heritage railways relied on the good grace, generosity and favour of a precious few wealthy fellows to provide the means to push and pull their meagre acquisitions of second hand, deteriorating tatty trucks and carriages. Parallel with growing demand for reliable locomotion, there inevitably became a shortage of working and reliable locomotives, exacerbated by the best restored and most attractive engines clamouring for attention on the main lines. It was a classic chicken and egg syndrome, and most heritage railways struggled to find enough working steam engines to run regularly and successfully, the Great Central included. Most relied on their revenue from galas where they borrowed each others stock. Today, this predicament prevails with ever more preserved lines opening up, even though there are many more locomotives available. The more established "Premier League" of railways rules the game though, with the GCR at the top of that tree being able to call on a fleet of eight home loco's to choose from. But it was not so back in 1978...

David Clarke and I had become close friends by the mid-

1970s. Since I came back from Africa in 1965 and had taken up my role at Ford and Slater, I had sought to do business with his family enterprise – Clarkes Boxes – of which he was a director. They were, at the time, the largest manufacturer of cardboard boxes in Europe. But I never did sell them any trucks, quite the reverse actually; I was to end up buying a number of vehicles from his Graypaul Motors Ferrari franchise. In all I bought eight Ferraris, all of which, I might add, when the time came, I sold at a handsome profit.

David and I could well have been brothers, if you take a look at our backgrounds. He was born in 1930 into a thriving Leicestershire family business and during David's childhood his father had been a pioneer 'petrol head' owning a Brooklands Delage 1920s Grand Prix racing car and several of the best Jaguars on the market. In his late teens, unlike me, David had tried his hand at motor racing and in 1950 broke the 500 lap record at Goodwood first time out in a Norton 500 engine road racer. He admitted though that the record didn't stand for long. In the final, in which he finished third, it fell to Stirling Moss in his new Kieft. A string of seconds and thirds followed, but after one season he packed in formula three racing citing that those single seater 500s back in those days were pretty abominable things to drive. He then tried his hand at longer distance car racing, firstly in a Frazer Nash Le Mans Replica acquired from his friend Bob Gerard. In mid 1951 he entered The Goodwood Nine Hours, the famous Le

Mans 24 hours race as co-driver to Bob Gerard, the Tourist Trophy, the British Empire Trophy and other long distance races at home and abroad. He usually drove the Gerard Frazer Nash finding these to be much more rewarding and successful than driving the temperamental Norton 500 vehicles. Variety came in the 1953 season when, from his base at Gerard's garage, he raced Gerard's ERAs, Cooper-Bristols, and the Le Mans replicas. He was asked in 1954 to test drive for Frank Raymond Wilton, head of the Jaguar Racing Team who was choosing works drivers for the 1954 Le Mans D-types. But instead, he chose to retire from racing because he was required to join the board of the family business which prevented him being a full-time racing driver quoting, "…as I don't like doing things by halves I didn't want to mess around as an amateur."

With his racing career finished, David decided on something more adventurous than just a nine-to-five job in the family business. He chose to learn film making and worked his way through all the essential jobs part time, up to that of producer. He then set up his own company making various films: motor racing, industrial, public relations, staff training and advertising coupled with responsibility for BBC and ATV newsreel coverage of motor sport throughout the Midlands. He graduated to 35 mm cinema feature filming, which included shooting all the action at Le Mans in 1960, for the film The Green Helmet, on an MGM commission. However, family ties being unbreakable, as I myself well know, the death of his uncle obliged him to rejoin the family business, bringing an end to his film making in early 1960.

His love of fast cars endured and he bought a 1951 Ferrari 212 Export, with Vignale drop-head coupé body, in late 1960. Helped by his old racing mechanic, Charles Jayes, who was still Clarke's Boxes Chief Engineer on cars and transport, he rebuilt the 212 in two years during his spare time. That first adventure into Ferraris proved to be the beginning of Graypaul Motors, which he started in 1971 out of a row of 4 garages adjacent to the Clarke's Boxes Factory in Mountsorrel. He soon outgrew this and bought further premises in Halstead Road, Mountsorrel, which is where he and I first met. He moved on from there to The Coneries in Loughborough. With such close interests and backgrounds we found a common bond and on most Saturdays, when I was in Leicestershire from about 1975 onwards, I would spend a few hours with David discussing motors and motor engineering over coffee and cigars – and at times donning overalls in the workshop on Halstead Road to tinker about on his latest acquisition.

It was on one such Saturday in 1978 that I talked to David about the GCR and the share offering available as it became a Public Limited Company. Until then he had had no real interest in the Great Central Railway as he was a devout Great Western Railway enthusiast. I have discovered over the years, a fierce partisan attitude usually prevails amongst enthusiasts and the more enthusiastic the follower the fiercer is that manifestation of "My passion is greater than thine..." David's railway fundamentalism came from the time he had spent with an uncle on his mother's side, who had been a signalman on the Great Western Railway whilst David was growing up.

Perhaps it's like a virus, or a disease, this railway enthusiasm that grabs so many? I can't say that I was ever interested in railways, trains, railway architecture, its paraphernalia or all the other facets that seem to infect the waves of humanity which flock line side all over the country whenever there's a trail of smoke, a whiff of steam or a toot and a clank in the near distance. At that time David and I both lived within the sound of the newly formed heritage railway and maybe it's the distant whistle or the beat of an engine when the wind is in the right direction that throws us back to our childhoods? Travelling by train then always meant an adventure away from the humdrum of everyday life. Who was it that said, 'Nostalgia isn't what it used to be?'

And so it came to pass that slowly and surely David became hooked and the pair of us spent more and more time, effort, influence and money upon the blessed born again GCR. Then one day I floated an idea past him, saying, "Hey, shall we buy a steam engine?"

"What?"

"You know - a railway locomotive."

"Erm - tell me more…"

So I explained that in my role at Unilever I had been contacted by one of our suppliers, Agfa Gevaert, who knew I was a shareholder of the GCR. They were a large creditor of a company that had gone into liquidation and had security on an asset that my contact thought I might be interested in. In lieu of the debt they were owed they had title to a British Railways 1934 built Jubilee class steam locomotive that had been fully restored.

I had to use all of my persuasive powers to bring David round to buying a London Midland and Scottish engine. If it had been a Great Western engine – a Hall, Manor, Grange or a Castle class, he would have snapped my hand off. I talked him round by reminding him that the designing engineer had been born at the Great Western town of Swindon and had been apprenticed to the greatest of Great Western loco designers Churchward - and that did the trick.

Not that we had any boxes to tick back in 1977 but this engine would, for me, have ticked them all. It had been a stalwart in all the years of steam since my birth. Designed by that most famous railway engineer Sir William Stanier, it was first introduced in 1934 and modified in 1937 – the year I was born – to become a common sight, hauling freight and passenger express services on all regions of British Rail right up to the withdrawal of steam locomotion in the 1960s. I bet there isn't an infected train spotter from those halcyon days anywhere in the length and breadth of our sacred island, whose pulse hasn't quickened at the sight and sound of a Stanier Jubilee. They were named to commemorate the Silver Jubilee of King George V and Queen Mary in 1935, the grand parents of our present queen. There were a hundred and ninety one of them built, many of them in our own East Midland region's premier railway works at Derby. All of them stayed in service past the nationalisation of the railways in 1948. The first to be withdrawn was number 5637 Windward Islands in1952 and only then because, having been the loco at the head one of the trains involved in the Harrow and Wealdstone disaster, it was damaged beyond repair. The Jubilees were the last Stanier-designed express passenger locomotives in service on BR, the final three lasting almost to the end of steam in 1967. When we bought Leander in 1978 there was only one other Jubilee that had been preserved, and that was Bahamas which resided at good old Dinting Railway centre – which you'll hear a little more of as my story moves on.

The first correspondence I have in the Leander file is dated 20th November 1977 from a well respected ex-British Railways locomotive engineering inspector by the name of Jack Street. It is an outline report on the state of Leander and advises that overall, the engine is in good condition but that we would do well to get a reduction in the price to reflect that a slight fracture had been found in the boiler.

The second item of correspondence is again from Jack Street and concludes with the recommendation that we should purchase Galatea, a sister engine to Leander, for its boiler spares. Galatea was languishing in Dai Woodham's scrap yard at Barry Docks in South Wales. Dai Woodham should be beatified as the patron saint of preserved heritage railways. He single-handedly reprieved more than 200 British Railway steam engines from the cutters' flame, this number representing about a fifth of all engines in steam today. Although he would have made a lot more money by cutting them up for scrap instead of hanging on to them until a buyer or a group could be found to restore them. He received an MBE in 1987, not for the steam engines he'd saved, but for job creation in South Wales after the pits had closed.

The asking price for the purchase of Leander was £55,000. And the price for the scrap condition Galatea was £8,910 – only a portion of what it would be worth as scrap metal at the market price per ton in 1977. If any doubt remained with David Clarke, it all evaporated when he first saw Leander at Dinting Railway Centre, Glossop, in the Peak District of Derbyshire.

There follow dozens of letters, back and forth to me and David, from all sorts of entities – Agfa Gevaert Limited, Moss Toone and Dean - Solicitors, Flying Scotsman Enterprises, Dinting Railway Centre, Woodham Bros. of Barry, South Wales, Wm. F. Prior & Co - Solicitors, Stewart Wrightson

(Northern) Limited - Insurers, H. M. Customs and Excise and the Vat Main Office to name but a few...

The locomotive was being looked after by staff and volunteers at the Dinting organisation who had spent time and money on its upkeep. They objected very strongly to the possibility of the engine being taken away from them, feeling they had a right to hang on to it for some reason. Obviously, the Dinting crowd was very far gone in the railway disease mentioned earlier...

Eventually, sometime in the summer of 1978, David and I, through a company we had set up called The Leander Locomotive Company Limited, became owners of Leander, although we had to leave her in the care of Dinting until the end of 1979, together with a donation of £2,500 to calm them down a bit.

Now, there is a lesson here for all who are passionate about our preserved railways: Dinting closed down in 1990 - no doubt because members couldn't agree on ways forward and funding options. The property was sold to a group of Manchester solicitors who were then refused planning permission, so now the whole site has gone to rack and ruin. It is over run with weeds, graffiti and decay. If you look on Google now for Dinting you will see one of railway preservation's saddest set of photographs. It is hard for me to imagine that was where we first set eyes on that most inspiring of sights – Leander in her original Crimson Lake livery...

We knew very well the expense we could expect, which goes with the ownership of something as big and heavy as that, and to pay for it we were going to create lots of imaginative merchandise that visitors would buy: mugs, framed photos, tea towels, lapel badges, caps, jigsaws, embroidered and monogrammed apparel and so on. We had seen it with the Flying Scotsman, owned and operated by Nottinghamshire businessman Alan Pegler, and we were pretty sure that we could create a 'Leander effect' which would pay handsomely. Our grand plan had been to make an 'Orient Express' kind of attraction, exclusively for the GCR, by funding a rake of First Class dining saloons, bringing visitors, cash and massive interest long before anyone else on any heritage railway in the UK. Both David and I were now directors of the GCR PLC, being the two largest independent shareholders, and we felt certain that our proposal to pay for Leander would meet with approval. We, of course, offered the engine for full and unfettered use on the GCR and even offered to donate half of the profit from the merchandising and catering to the railway's coffers.

We were turned down flat.

We should not have been surprised. We had seen the Dinting lot and how precious they were about everything with their skewed perspective of ownership, revenue, cost and expense. In those days there were very few owner agreements in place on any railway and just about the only place you could get any pay back was by running tours and excursions on British Rail. We were being far too innovative for the day. Profit, or anything akin to making one, from something as precious as this Great Central Religion was tantamount to heresy and any plan that uttered such a possibility seemed like blasphemy. Okay, I'm being a bit sarcastic here, but in many quarters of volunteer organisations this spirit is endemic.

David and I could not understand the lack of foresight shown by the collective board in 1979, when Leander had fully come into our possession. Their official statement read something like this:

"It is not permissible for shareholders, directors, officers or others associated with the railway to be receiving commercial financial gain from the running of rolling stock or locomotives on the privately run Great Central Heritage lines."

I do think, now, that a lot of this short sighted attitude was naivety. Common sense took a while to evolve but, a year or two after the Leander saga, owner agreements did come about which paid owners of engines and rolling stock either per mile or per steaming day. And pretty soon the railways were getting busier with paying visitors and everyone could see that the railway would be served better the more attractions there were for people to enjoy.

But that initial reception dampened our enthusiasm considerably, so we funded our engine from excursions on the main line. Over more than a decade of our ownership of both engines, we made a home for Leander and Galatea at the Severn Valley Railway at Bridgenorth. The team there took it upon themselves to rebuild Galatea, engineering new parts where needed. Bob Meanly, my oldest friend from traction engine days, was on side and willing to lead the group as Chief Mechanical Engineer, being responsible for maintenance and project managing the careful swapping of spare parts from Galatea as and when Leander would need them. Leander never came back to the GCR whilst in our ownership, which makes me sad even today when I think about it.

Nevertheless, David and I had numerous trips on the footplate up and down the main lines of England, Wales and Scotland - we could never have done that without Leander. I met some terrific people on those trips, hard working, dedicated men, proud of their skills, who, I could see first hand, absolutely loved the work and all that it entailed. I came to know, much more than I had ever felt with the traction engines I had owned along with my father, the life power that an engine like Leander had to give. I understood that she needed to be coaxed, nursed and cajoled to bring out her best when needed. I experienced the awesome power she could wield. I just had to look behind, out of the open cab window, at the 13 coach train with five hundred passengers on board, in all getting on for a five hundred ton payload, gliding as smooth as silk as we approached the Shap incline to the highest summit on the

British Railway system, racing along at seventy or eighty miles an hour. The excitement was palpable in the extreme. Man and machine in perfect harmony. This was one of the most powerful types of land machine ever built in England in the history of mankind up to the nineteen fifties.

You may have been asking why we wanted to get involved at this level, especially with all the resistance, negative attitudes, jealousy and Luddite ignorance that seemed to pervade everything to do with bringing railways back to life. In a nutshell, I could say the reason was found on that footplate whilst steaming up the Great Western main line to Scotland. David referred to the GWR as God's Wonderful Railway and during that precious time I spent with or without him on the footplate of Leander through the Lancashire and Cumbrian countryside I thought the same. In my lifetime, those hours I have spent on the footplate are equal to any of the hours I have enjoyed flying my planes or driving my fast cars on clear open roads. It's the nearest thing I know of where art and science combine to produce something amazing, something truly sublime.

But I chose to step away from direct involvement with the GCR for the next few years. Achieving success when part of the process requires bashing one's head against hard and immovable surfaces is not for the faint-hearted (or headed for that matter) and I was needed elsewhere in the world, as you have already read. And, even though I was a wealthy man back in those days, I could see how something like the GCR would evaporate money in no time. No wonder the governments of the 1960s were keen to get rid of as many track miles as they could, as fast as they could. The costs involved in bringing merely one engine back to life were phenomenal: having to make new parts from scratch because the original drawings had disappeared and the materials needed to make them were scarce and costly. Then there was the infrastructure that was falling down before our eyes and the pie in the sky dreamers who insist on the absolutely correct hue of paint for a screw head in an old signal box or hinge on a ticket office cupboard. And finally, for now, there was David Clarke, with his dream of re-instating part of the Great Central to double track between Loughborough and Rothley. He always was a bigger dreamer than me, but he had a fair bit more in the bank as well!

History shows how David's dreams played out, finally getting them to reality with the official opening of the double track main line on June 1st 2000. And him pulling the lever in Rothley signal box to give the "right-away" to the first engine, Witherslack Hall, (at last a Great Western engine in his charge!) to leave Rothley on the new Down Main line to Loughborough.

But once that invasive railway mania bug had truly bitten him, his attention moved on from Leander to grander schemes and over time he wasn't as interested in a "lowly" engine really. By the end of 1990, Leander was out of service, with a refurbishment needed before she would be allowed to run anywhere again; rusting away, lying idle in a weed infested siding at Bridgnorth in Shropshire on the Severn Valley Railway. David and I had dissolved the Leander Company and we had written the engine down to zero as a tax loss.

I was living in the Isle of Man by then when I was contacted by Michael Draper who was the General Manager of the Severn Valley Railway. They were interested in restoring Leander back to running order, using the engineering facilities available at Bridgnorth. Michael Draper, although he had clearly been infected by Railway Malaise at some point in his life, had adapted and become a Preservation Railway Professional. He was a man with a lot of common sense and a realistic attitude about engines, volunteers and the need for commercialisation in order to pay the ever present bills. Michael had agreed a total price for the refurbishment of £150,000, and envisaged a return to working order of about eighteen months. I was all prepared to pay the fees to get Leander back up to running order and then go it alone, as David had moved on to other projects, and I was happy to leave the engine in Severn Valley Railway's care as a thank you for all the work and attention the engine would receive. Unfortunately, right in the middle of our negotiations, I suffered the brain haemorrhage I told you about in chapter 16 and this brought an end to all of my involvement from that point on.

During my convalescence a Doctor Beet, along with his son, showed an interest in Leander and having decided to let the engine go, I transferred ownership for a nominal sum. Michael Draper and the Severn Valley Railway had kept their word and restored the loco to running condition which enabled the sale to proceed. I suppose you could say that I had had my fussy out by owning an engine, but more especially because I was now officially domiciled in the Isle of Man and was not allowed to own property or any new assets in England.

Leander did eventually grace the Great Central's rails in the Autumn gala of 2008. She now resides at Carnforth where ownership has passed to Dr Beet's son.

David Clarke, through his dream and his legacy, will live on for as long as the Great Central Railway survives. He died on the 27th July, 2002 on a steam hauled first class dining train on the double track section of Great Central Railway after enjoying a five course lunch at the Summer Gala - the big hearted man whose heart failed him at the last at the age of seventy two. It was after David died that I set up a trust in his name to preserve the funds and the legacy he left for the good of all who love railways, especially the Great Central.

I don't possess the ability to dream like David did. But I can manage a company. And for the following fourteen years that's what I did. The first seven years by guaranteeing bank overdrafts, negotiating terms with owners of engines and getting new funders on board; then taking up the reins officially from 2007 when I became chairman and managing director. As much as I would not want to admit that I had caught this all consuming addiction, I find no other explanation that answers the question as to why I got involved at all, never mind to the extent that I did.

I'll set down more fully in my last chapter the answer to 'Where do we go from here?' But for now, I rest my interest in that blessed enterprise with younger persons and those with more money than me.

And here's a fitting end to this chapter and my life story so far: A couple of weeks ago my youngest daughter Julia, was invited on a main line rail excursion by one of the staff from the GCR. Julia had worked for the railway for a couple of years up to the beginning of 2017. She had been told that it was Leander that was to be hauling the train during the day but it turned out to be Galatea, the engine that would never have been restored at all had David Clarke and I not bought her for spares nearly forty years ago.

★   ★   ★

A lot of knowledge can be a dangerous thing and danger-
ously boring. Often I have leapt up from the perusal of a
railway book and cried "If only this chap knew less and told
me more!"

From the introduction to 'Steaming through Britain'
by Miles Kington

Chapter 19

Forward Leaning

Books on the history of The Great Central Railway are legion and better men than I have dealt out the detail down to the last splinter from an old rotting sleeper, so this version will not be competing with those at any level.

Until the late autumn of 1975 I had no involvement and no more than a lay person's passing interest in what was happening with the defunct railway line that ran through our green and pleasant countryside. Then, out of the blue, two young men came to visit me at Ford & Slater's offices on Narborough Road Leicester. They were Richard Lovatt and Graham Oliver and they wanted to see if I would be interested in investing in this new OLD venture - the Great Central Railway. Richard and Graham walked away with a cheque for £1000 and I thought no more of it until the following spring when British Rail, refusing to be convinced that a purchase would ever be made, started planning the line's dismemberment. I was asked if I would go to London with Richard & Graham to the head office of British Rail at Marylebone to have one last go at a stay of execution. The bid was now for the line between Loughborough and Quorn stations, including just one of the two tracks.

The appointment was set up in deputy chairman Mr. Bobbie Lawrence's office at 09:00 on a Friday morning and the remaining track was due to be lifted for scrap on the following Monday. At the time, we were unaware that Mr. Lawrence had called the chief engineer at Derby immediately before our meeting with the instruction that whatever the outcome he was to remove the track on schedule on Monday morning.

£80k, in1976 terms, was still owed and a plan was put forward to pay £40k on Monday and the remaining £40k thirty days later. After some discussion this was agreed - but only after we'd assured Mr. Lawrence that he could keep the first £40k if the cheque for the second and final £40k was not forthcoming!

As we walked away across the station, Graham asked if I had £80k in the bank.

I said, "No, but we've got all day to raise it!"

At 10am I rang the then Eastern Regional Director of National Westminster bank, Mr. Neville Drane, who was based in Nottingham but had been Area Manager in Leicester. At that time our family firm's account was one of the long term, established growing businesses which had banked with Nat West for many years, commencing with the Westminster Bank in 1928. I asked Neville if I could borrow £80k, to which his immediate response was, "What do you want it for this time,

Bill?" Having explained that we had bought a railway he asked if I had dealt with the Leicester Area Manager of Nat West, Dennis Simpson, to which my response was, "No, I've come straight to the top in the hope that we could settle it together." He told me to write out two separate cheques for £40k on our normal GCR business account, the only request being that I visit the bank in the next week and sign a personal guarantee!

In fact I remained bank guarantor for several years. I joined the GCR board and took over as chairman from Richard Willis in August of that year. The early board needed in-depth business and financial knowledge so over the years up to 1984 I worked closely with Denis Butler, Earl of Lanesborough, whose estate was bisected by the GCR, until I had to resign to take up the job in Saudi Arabia.

Soon after David Clarke's death in 2003, I was approached by Graham Oliver to see if I could help. Nat West had frozen the GCR account, concerned about the ongoing losses as it was David's support that had kept the railway going. At that stage we'd not paid creditors for four and a half months, the overdraft was at its maximum of £100k and employees were being told not to put their pay cheques in the bank until the income from a weekend gala or special event had cleared. On the formation of the David Clarke Railway Trust, it was agreed that Malcolm Freckelton and I would represent the

Trust at board meetings.

Eventually, after my time living abroad and in the Isle of Man, I returned to England to help save GCR (1976) plc Ltd. which meant losing my Inheritance Tax cover.

In 2006 Richard Lovatt was diagnosed with aggressive cancer and sadly passed away in 2007 with me at his bedside in Leicester Royal Infirmary.

It was at this point in 2007 that I took over the reins of that unwieldy, unruly and expensive collection of chariots of fire; if I had known then what I know now, would I have taken it on? As I have shown in the chapter on Lord Lanesborough, it can be a thankless and unrewarding task. There's not even the comfortable satisfaction to be gained - as there can be in many underpaid vocations such as nursing, caring, religious orders, etc. - that Heaven might be your reward at the end; although there are a few who envisage David Clarke looking down from on high. Actually, if you visit Lovatt House anytime soon, look up to your right as you walk through the first set of inner doors into the reception corridor and you'll see a sculpture of his head looking down on you from a little shelf in a corner. But let me just say, Lovatt House isn't Heaven, not by a long chalk; some say that a Tasmanian devil once worked there. Read on!

The word *languishing* could have first been penned to describe the state of much of the GCR's inventory which I took over in 2007. As I have always done when starting in earnest on a new challenge, I quickly identified where to get the most impact, in the fastest time, at an affordable price. This time it was to be from a *languishing* BR Standard 7F Britannia Pacific class of locomotive which was owned by the National Railway Museum (NRM) - 70013 Oliver Cromwell. I had a good idea of what would be involved from my experience with Leander and Galatea, so I wasn't surprised when I started moving and shaking the various factions that would be needed to help restore the wonderful Britannia to full working order. The pedigree of this locomotive cannot be under estimated. In some ways it deserves as much adulation as that star of wonder 4472 The Flying Scotsman (its present number is 60103) and in some enthusiast circles it gets top ranking above even that. Oliver Cromwell was the last steam engine to be overhauled at Crewe by British Railways, the last standard gauge engine to receive a name and it was the last working, British Railway owned, steam engine to haul passenger trains of any description on main lines in 1968 - because good old BR had banned all privately owned steam loco's from working on main lines.

Sunday August 11th 1968 was the final curtain for scheduled steam-hauled traction and Oliver Cromwell was chosen to haul the Manchester Victoria to Carlisle section of the last BR steam train "The Fifteen Guinea Special". It was so called because of the high price of a ticket - £260 at 2018 value.

After being withdrawn, Cromwell languished lovingly at Bressingham Steam Museum in Norfolk, on "permanent loan" from the NRM, being steamed only for high days and holidays until 1973. It then fell silent for twenty years, until in 1993 a group of afflicted enthusiasts, having raised tens of thousands of pounds to restore Cromwell to its former glory, challenged Bressingham's title to hold on to the engine. There was a bitter feud which ended with the engine staying at the Norfolk site and all those that had donated receiving their money back. It took another ten years before that dog-in-a-manger stalemate could be broken and only then because Bressingham were offered another ennobled engine, class V2 2-6-2 4771 Green Arrow, as a replacement.

Fund raising began again in earnest and in the summer of 2004 Cromwell arrived at Loughborough shed in readiness for an overhaul at an estimated cost in the region of a hundred thousand pounds. Progress from 2004 was slow, but this is so often the case with heritage volunteer enterprises. Underestimating is one of the biggest hold ups to these projects and the biggest shortfall is always the cost of materials and expert labour. The best and most enthusiastic will in the entire world cannot match a professional expert and there are always insufficient resources to match the passion. The converse is also true. Overestimating is the professional's folly – look at HS2 and the like. As you read on you will see how the GCR has also become a victim of this pernicious condition. Both need careful management and astute scrutiny to find the path to victory – and to the right price!

By 2007 a groundswell of fevered interest had grown in railway circles, whipped up by the enthusiasts' magazines, to re-create the Fifteen Guinea Special and to use Cromwell as one of the locos to haul it, again over the Settle and Carlisle route, on the 40th anniversary of the official end of steam-hauled passenger trains.

When I took over the reins, it was clear to me that Cromwell was the key to the immediate future. I met with the teams and people engaged in the restoration, keeping managers and directors at the NRM informed of our progress. I gave the NRM my personal assurance, rashly, that the engine would be ready to steam again in time for the 40th anniversary special.

Early on in my management career I had learned the value of sharp and succinct language, used sparingly, to get things done. Tom Tighe had been the chief mechanical engineer at Loughborough leading the team restoring the engine. Tom himself was a confirmed exponent of sharp and succinct communication! Time was ticking by and I was getting extremely nervous that my promise to the NRM would not be honoured. Those who have come to know me will attest that I am not the most convivial of colleagues when deadlines are nearing and failure is looming. I asked Tom a few weeks before the deadline if Cromwell would be ready in time and his reply was rather vague saying, "It'll be done when it's done." That really infuriated me! Since then the engineering teams at Loughborough have nicknamed me 'Taz' - short for Tasmanian devil - although not within my earshot.

The Tasmanian devil then asked Craig Stinchcombe to take over and I let it be known that the job *would* be finished on time and bonuses *would* be forthcoming. I often turned up after hours, travelling back from home in Kibworth Harcourt with fish and chip suppers for them as they worked round the clock shifts, seven days a week, to complete.

I know there were a number of those that helped on the restoration who didn't agree with some of my methods or my ethics, perhaps being at odds with the spirit of volunteering, but let history be my judge.

Cromwell was an unmitigated triumph for the GCR; she became our flagship engine and helped to forge our reputation for getting things done, creating trust and a reverence for us throughout the heritage railway industry. The original estimate proved to be out by more than a factor of three, the final cost being £324,000. The David Clarke Trust, of which I was still chairman, gave £90,000, Steam Railway gave a total of £84,000, the NRM a total of £12,000 and the balance was paid in full by 5305 LA from passenger income received.

It had not escaped my notice that the name of the engine was not too dissimilar to a certain booming Leicestershire business with its HQ just south of Leicester. I visited Michael Gregory, principal shareholder and CEO of Cromwell Tools, at his office in Wigston on many occasions during my time at the GCR and it's no coincidence that these visits commenced sometime around the summer of 2007. Subsequently Michael became a great friend and benefactor to the railway and remains the principal individual funder to this day. Without Michael Gregory the railway would not be anywhere near as viable as it is now, if indeed it would be viable at all.

Once Cromwell was completed on time and our reputation was secured, I set about looking into the really big dream – joining up the two halves of the remaining GCR. I formed a team to look at the project with partners of Network Rail, Charnwood and Rushcliffe Borough Councils, Leicester City and County Councils, together with the two railways in question – GCR Nottingham and us. We found funding to appoint Atkins Consulting to create a case for the Greater Great Central Railway. A year later they came up with a document that identified the feasibility of connecting the two halves with a bridge over the Midland Main Line near the Brush Works just north of Loughborough Midland Station.

I have to hand it to these professionals, and I sometimes think that my father was right all those decades ago when he wanted me to go and get a university education, because if you really want to make money for little material outlay, just become a consultant! We were charged £75,000 for a 136 page report. They dreamed up new schemes within the grand scheme with eight different possibilities. We at the GCR, north and south, were really only concerned with the connection and, if truth be known, it was us in the south that needed the connection, for the north were quite happy as they were as they already had a connection to the main line for trains to access the gypsum works at East Leake. For us, joining up to the north meant that we also would have direct rail connection to Network Rail. In the twenty first century that link to Network Rail is vital in unlocking the potential for excursions on and off our railway from all over the kingdom, together with a much lower cost and a method of transport with less risk of damage for visiting loco's in and out of our railway system. All but three of their eight proposed possibilities were dismissed by Atkins as not commercially viable.

Do you see an irony here? They create possibilities and research them at great expense, only to dismiss them in the final analysis. We could have told them that in the first place, but I guess no one did. Incidentally, the total cost of all the work proposed, as Atkins had presented it, was £95.5 million.

From July 2009, when the report was first published, two of the projects were set in motion, the honey trap of National Lottery funding was triggered and there ensued frantic PR from all sides.

It was around this time that I appointed Kate Tilley as our marketing manager. She built a team that set the railway on the road to becoming the East Midlands premier tourist attraction. Kate did not achieve this alone, but instigated new ideas to develop our concept as a theme park. She was in control when the turnover increased from £1.7 million in 2009 to £3 million in 2016.

Steve Cramp led the way with the Mountsorrel branch line project after the Atkins proposal, securing sizeable funding, separately, from LaFarge-Tarmac and the National Lottery. He succeeded in getting the line completed in record time although it is my belief that the whole railway would have been better and faster served if that project had been integrated into the bridge at Loughborough project. But Steve had momentum in his favour and he and his team steamrollered their way to success and never looked back - until he wanted a connection to the main GCR line at Swithland. His fundraising and momentum didn't stretch as far as that and fell a few hundred thousand pounds short, causing inevitable delays in connecting up. In 2018 we are still waiting. Certainly, he saw his opportunity and ran with it. I was impressed with what he achieved and I did recommend him to the board to take over my job when I retired, but he turned it down.

This is an example of the difficulty faced by whoever is at the helm of something like the GCR. There are dozens of different projects simmering away all the time and it is nigh-on impossible to co-ordinate them into a common way forward. The result being that one favoured project can get all the attention and funding, turning focus and resources away from the longer term potential of the railway. I suppose the phrase "he who shouts the loudest will be listened to" is true here.

Tom Ingle spearheaded the promotion for the bridge and did a fantastic job leading the fundraising, producing media collateral and pushing the message far and wide. He coined the name "Bridge to the Future" which really did tick all the boxes perfectly.

Lili Taberner had been recommended to me by Peter Soulsby, elected Mayor of Leicester, and Lili led the creation of the bid to the National Lottery.

I believe we went too far with our enthusiasm for the lottery. We should not have flattered ourselves in thinking we could project manage the Bridge to the Future at the same time as the museum at Birstall. But, as I have often said, hindsight is a truly wonderful thing and serves no one any good after the event, except in the writing of history books. I did push my opinion strongly that the railway and the museum should always be separate entities with separate management. When Andy Munro took over at the GCR the management were joined together. Therein lies the folly and the reason the lottery dropped their interest, stalling all work on the Connection to the Future project.

But, as an organisation, we were grossly unprepared for the change required to absorb what was needed to receive sizable lottery funding. The impetus created by Network Rail's announcement in July 2012 that the Midland Main Line electrification was going ahead, meant that if we were to build a bridge we would have to do it before the electrification work was started. It was a "now or never" scenario.

We appointed FJD Civil Engineering Consulting Group as our Civil Engineers. The main shareholder of FJD was working on contract for Network Rail when the Government agreed to the electrification programme north of Bedford to Derby and he also headed a team put together by NR to head up HS2. Any conflict of interest was accepted by NR. In discussion with NR at Derby a team was put together under the auspices of Spencer Gibbens, the civil engineering public relations consultant, to work as a community project between NR and GCR. The purpose of this was to show people in the area that NR were doing positive things to help the local community and thus make it easier to proceed. Upgrading bridges and the like would cause country lane road closures all the way along the line from Bedford to Derby and local opinion needed managing all along the route. Ten railway managers from Network Rail volunteered to bring their expertise on a voluntary basis to help achieve our goals. Meetings were held at Derby, one at Cromwell Tools and the rest at GCR Loughborough. The target figure for fund raising at that time was £1,000,000. It was hoped that the successful bridge installation would ensure that NR continued to give us full support to complete the embankment and to install another two bridges. We had possession of two bridges which Spencer Gibbens and his team had procured via Nigel Harris, long time GCR supporter, director and railway journalist. The bridges had seen life on Network Rail near Reading, Berkshire until 2010 when the line there was upgraded. They have been in our ownership since then, and lay on land next to Loughborough GCR station for several years. They are now stored for safe keeping by Allelys, our heavy haulage contractor. It was expected that within two years they would be needed but they are still not installed eight years later.

When the funding had reached approximately £750,000 in the early summer of 2015 the Midland Mainline electrification project was at first postponed and then cancelled altogether. At that stage some of our team ceased their involvement leaving Nigel Harris, Lili Taberner, Michael Firth and myself to manage things.

We called a meeting at Network Rail's office in Derby. Before the electrification cancellation we had confirmed and agreed that our contribution would be £1.19 million. Now that the project was stalled Network Rail rescinded their agreement to help with work and funding. The meeting was extremely fraught. To rescue the situation I asked Spencer Gibbens what the cost would be to have Network Rail work with us on a commercial basis. The regional senior engineer at Network Rail, Richard Walker, refused to give us a figure saying we could not afford it! I reminded him that it was his duty to give us a price, especially with the difficult circumstances they had left us in. I know I had put him on the spot and he did look uncomfortable trying to fob us off further, but he eventually came up with a firm price of £2.8 million.

The David Clarke Trust had £750,000 in the "Bridge to the Future" fund and there was another £3,000,000 in accounts for special projects – a good portion of that had come from Michael Gregory and two major legacies. But we still had the embankment to re-build, the connection to the bridge over Railway Terrace at the back of Precis Spark's factory and the canal bridge to deal with which hadn't seen any care or attention for more than 50 years. Before we started the "Bridge to the Future" fund it had been acknowledged by the board that if we could raise a million pounds we could go for money to install the other two bridges and the embankment as both shareholders and supporters would continue their support.

We approached several firms including Lafarge, Mixed Concrete and Waste Cycle. It was anticipated by Waste Cycle that if they accepted the contract and by working through Landfill Tax, at worst the contribution from GCR would be zero and at best we would have a rebate at the end of the project. The truck operators would pay the normal landfill fees and Waste Cycle would manage and operate the project and the site, as they had successful experience and were extremely professional (with a small "p"). They also anticipated that they could receive up to 2,000 tons capacity a day, on our behalf, in twenty ton tipper lorries. The embankment needed about a quarter of a million tons and therefore, in theory, if unlimited spoil was available we could have the bulk of the embankment in around three or four months.

As stated we had contracted FJD to ensure the specification of the product was as required, but that was never completed in my term of office, which was almost two years ago. That part of the project was abandoned at that point and to date has not been re-started. They did talk to Lafarge-Tarmac about the overburden which would only be suitable in small quantities due to its relatively unstable contents. Lafarge-Tarmac have been great supporters of GCR, donating thousands of tons of ballast to the Mountsorrel project and hundreds of tons of the highest spec ballast to GCR. We had an excellent business relationship with Phil Cox, the General Manager at Lafarge Mountsorrel and his team. The GCR has also had long term support from Tony Allsop, whose company supplies mixed concrete and who had allocated all the bridge concrete for "the Gap" at cost price, valid for a year. One of my last acts was to pass this over to the incoming Chief Executive Officer, Andy Munro. This was never followed up. All of that opportunity was lost and ought to be a lesson for those that now replace me. If you let the "Professionals" rule, (with a capital "P") expect to pay top prices for everything, they don't know how to negotiate. They are not businessmen. If I have

326

learned anything in life it is that the price written on the front of the package is always up for negotiation; that's the price which the seller will make his maximum profit on and is not necessarily a fair price.

I couldn't attend last year's Annual General Meeting of shareholders (I was quite ill and wrestling with the grim reaper, who thought I might be ready again – for the ninth time I think!) but I have been told by reliable sources of a hot topic on the agenda: "Where was the 20 million coming from to complete the connection to the northern section?"

It's amazing how rumours quickly become "fact".

The latest appeal, as at spring 2018, was to raise money for the repair of the bridge over the canal at the northern end of the Loughborough shed complex. Apparently, according to the Tom Ingle video that launched this part of the campaign at the end of November 2017, it is going to cost at least £475,000. Perhaps there is a little amount of expectation management going on here, maybe playing for time. But I would urge the new regime to heed my earlier warning to treat your customers and your colleagues with the utmost respect, for they are not fools, they will find you out and it will be to everyone's cost.

In 2015, once fundraising for the Bridge to the Future was in full swing we changed the make up of the GCR's civil engineering team. Until then we had too few experienced engineers, too many amateurs and we weren't moving on quickly enough with our plans. I had always known from the start that the biggest danger with a huge project like this was that we could be stuck in the middle with a bridge to nowhere. We had to have a firm plan where the railway was to run - through or around the shed complex. To move the shed could close the railway, costing extra millions we didn't need to spend, so the obvious route was to the west of the shed. Install a new single line by the existing buildings, continue on past the parking area and join up with the existing loop at the north end of Platform 2 on Loughborough Station. Of course, before the heritage railway came about, the main line ran right through the middle of where the shed is now.

The new team comprised of David Slack, who has a wealth of experience in civil engineering spanning more than 35 years, Graham Bannister who is probably the best signal and telegraph expert anywhere on heritage railways, Andrew Higginson who has headed up our Permanent Way team for many years now and me acting as chairman, which allowed decisions to be made quickly.

Consultations with Charnwood Borough council went smoothly and they agreed that the best route was the one we had outlined as there are no residents on that side of the land and it was likely there'd be no one new to complain about additional noise or smoke from engines. The cost we came up with was a realistic £2.5 million.

On Friday 12th February 2016 when Loughborough MP Nicky Morgan turned the first sod for the commencement of work to build the biggest dream anyone at the railway had ever seen, all the cards were in place for everything to roll on to finish with a realistic completion date of sometime in 2019. We had the money, the plan for the embankment at zero cost for the material, two bridges to help cross Railway Terrace behind Preci Spark and the momentum to carry us through. Agreements were in place with suppliers, contractors, councils and everyone necessary to succeed.

We were the darlings of the Heritage Railway industry, all eyes were on us and we had support from far and wide.

So, what happened?

Why, more than two years on, do we have a bridge that sits alone and is going nowhere anytime soon because apparently there is no planning permission or money to complete the dream? Is doing up a rusty old canal bridge all we can think of in order to move forward? Right now, in spring 2018, the GCR looks like a laughing stock. But the answer is quite simple really and yes, good old hindsight is at the ready again to slap us all across the face with a large wet fish!

Some of it is unfortunate circumstance, but most of it is down to a few individuals who have neglected their responsibilities. We, and that includes me, chose the wrong person to take over from me. After 10 days of accompanying him around the railway in July 2016 I knew he was the wrong man. I told the most senior members of our board exactly that but no one heeded.

A critical eye operation prevented me from attending the board meeting in August 2016 and I was ousted in my absence. How I was treated beggars belief. It had been put in writing that I was going to retire at the end of 2017, but this I was not allowed to do. I should have been allowed to project manage the Bridge to the Future on a part time basis, which was the plan all along, once I had recovered from the operation.

The museum project was absorbed into the bridge project and everything came to a standstill when the Heritage Lottery people pulled out. They pulled out because it was obvious that the management of all facets of the GCR was insufficient to sustain progress on all fronts at the same time.

The greatest folly, as I see it, is that the senior management as a whole shunned me and thought they could manage things on their own. I was asked by Michael Gregory to stay away from the railway to let things settle down and not to contact any of the senior personnel. Senior management and some of the new board threatened to report me for investigation by HMRC for financial irregularities relating to expenses claimed by me during my time as chairman and managing director. I sometimes claimed mileage allowance and took benefactors, suppliers, or consultants for lunch on occasion. I hope you can imagine the hurt and the anger this caused within me. I had worked tirelessly, seven days a week for most weeks, over nearly ten years, receiving not a penny in salary. In fact the total cost to me as an individual over that time amounts to more than £400,000. Having checked their threat out, I found that HMRC would never do anything without writing to the accused first. It was a clear case of biting the hand that feeds. For many months Munro was successful in turning almost everyone in a management position against me. As we all know, when it really matters and the chips are down, you can usually count your real friends on the fingers of one hand. And here, at this point in my book I would like to thank Mick Carr, Mike and Chris Lang, David Slack and Kate Tilley. They remained loyal and allowed me to pull through with a modicum of self respect.

I offered time and time again to help but no one wanted to know, or perhaps they couldn't swallow their pride. It was pitiful. Friends I'd known for years refused to have anything to do with me, as if I'd caught a dangerous infectious disease. Senior employees of the GCR were ordered not to contact me. "The King is dead, long live the King" might explain the actions of many who shunned me or perhaps they didn't think much of me anyway and it was me that got it wrong all along. But I was still alive and that was perhaps a bit of an inconvenience for some. It's a great shame that such a fabulous working life should end in such a distressing way. It almost killed me, but fortunately I was strong enough to survive and it gave me time to put my life experiences into written form.

However, momentum was lost which might never be regained. Munro resigned in May 2017 and the company was left floundering. Who knows what his agenda was? It certainly wasn't for the good of the whole.

The only trophy in all of this is that there is now a branch line to a quarry.

The railway has been set back 5 years and if the tide isn't turned soon all that will remain will be a bridge to nowhere and two 8 mile unconnected railway lines with a disintegrating infrastructure that even rich men can't fix. The Dinting effect is a stark reminder of how fragile all we have built together really is.

The very best time the railway has ever had was when everyone's dreams coincided. David Clarke's dual track dream pulled the railway out of the doldrums and turned the GCR into something very special. When I joined to run the show in 2007 we were still riding on the crest of that wave and we capitalised on it; with careful choices of the right people in the right jobs we turned the railway into a premier profitable attraction. When we launched the Bridge to the Future we stepped up a couple of gears and really started to steam; everyone was on board with the common aim of connecting the two halves. We allowed ourselves to be entangled with Lottery money but if we could have kept the dream alive we would have survived and succeeded. But Munro derailed us, and there was no one there to put us back on the tracks.

How can it be fixed?

Re-light the fire of that burning dream everyone understands. And it has to be soon.

I remain very proud of what I was able to do for all those that consider the GCR a part of their lives, however small – customers on a day trip, volunteers on the footplate, in a canteen or Pullman dining car, collectors on a train or a steward on a Santa Train.

In my time we have transformed the business of the GCR through marketing, catering, engineering and sound day to day management. We raised in excess of £10 million in donations for various projects and we nearly made it to become the very best in the business; all we needed was that connection. But I just couldn't get to that final bridge before they shut off my steam.

As I have said before, it is by far the hardest job I have ever done.

If I were a younger man would I do it all again?

No.

The cost in human terms, for me, was too much.

Never mind the money…

★   ★   ★

Afterwords

It was customary on leaving Stowe that entries were made by your friends in the hymn book - Cantata Stoica - that each boy was given when he started at the school.

Together with a quote my school friend Michael Gawer sketched this pencil drawing of me at the point in my life when I was about to leave Stowe school at the age of 18 and begin my apprenticeship with Vauxhall.

Team Work

by Bill Ford

Over the last twenty years or so many people have said that I should put my life experiences in written form and at the end of 2016, when my business world had collapsed and I was suddenly cast aside, I realised the time had come to write them down, beginning with my earliest memories in 1940.

Obviously the key person in my project would be the editor or guiding light. Initially I worked with a railway friend, Richard Tilden Smith, but after he moved from the Midlands to the south of England, meetings became almost impossible to schedule in on a weekly basis.

Several people had recommended Steve Johns to me and, arranging to meet him for lunch, it was obvious to me that luck was on my side. So much of our lives had followed similar patterns that we immediately moved into a positive working relationship and I am 100% convinced that the decisions we took then were the right ones.

Steve's knowledge in the writing and editing of my story has been exceptional and he has chosen some perfect quotations to enhance the facts. I said at the beginning that I did not want anything but the truth to be told and I have stuck rigidly to that format. Fortunately, my memory remains excellent and I have resisted all temptation to exaggerate.

I have probably burdened Steve too much, but our trust and friendship has grown. I am certain I could not have done this on my own and equally sure that the partnership between us is the best available. I take this opportunity to say "Thank you Steve for all your help."

★   ★   ★

The Journey of Writing the Book
by Steve Johns

On the 21st March 2017, when Bill Ford and I first sat down for lunch at the Quorndon Fox to discuss the opportunity for me to be involved in writing his memoirs, there were few people on earth whom I had met that I held in higher esteem. Our imaginations are often not accurate when we put them to measuring someone we do not know, especially someone we have put on a pedestal like I had done with Bill Ford. But, I didn't know him then. For sure I knew what he had achieved, first hand for the most part in my role as an active volunteer on the GCR. An old adage suggests that knowledge might be a dangerous thing, therefore has my esteem diminished over the last year, since I have got to know such a lot more about him?

Shortly into our meeting, after he had begun to précis some of the main points of his life, a phrase popped into my head and I wrote, in quotation marks: "A Life on Fire".

At that time I didn't know the background as to why he had left his position as managing director of the GCR. Along with most of the rest of the staff and volunteers, I followed the line that he had retired and that was that. What Bill told me about that debacle truly shocked me and it was apparent that he was deeply affected by the way he had been ousted and had indeed suffered ill health as a direct result of what had happened - or more to the point how it had happened. He told me of his state of health, that he had had prostate cancer for the last 15 years and he made it very clear that if we were going to write this book together we had better get on with it.

He astounded me with his tales of brushes with the grim reaper and I counted at least 6 lives he'd had – the Austin Healey crash, the Kilimanjaro folly, landing a plane on a motorway in a monsoon, being confronted head on by a bull elephant on the Masia Mara, a brain haemorrhage, prostate cancer and we were only a half an hour into our first meeting!

I knew it would be a big task to co-write this book and collaborative writing was something I had never attempted before. Also, I was now the co-owner and joint editor of a successful and growing local magazine and had limited time to embark on a project of this magnitude. To do it justice I reckoned that I would need to visit Bill and spend two to three hours listening to his story at least three times a month and then spend at least one full day after each session writing up on my notes. It would take at least the rest of the year to write sufficient content in order to produce a publishable memoir.

I did have a head start with the notes taken by Richard Tilden Smith, who had begun the writing process with Bill the previous October. Richard's notes have been invaluable, especially in the early stages, and have helped verify a lot of the detail. I knew that I couldn't see this to fruition unless the task sat right with me in all respects and there was a degree of compensation for the time I could not spend on other aspects of my busy life. I knew I would have to reduce my involvement as a volunteer at the GCR and forgo some of my weekend time with Mary. One of the earliest things I realised was that Bill Ford is an extremely pragmatic, realistic and generous man. Not having any idea of the going rate for co-writing services I felt happy at going forward with just my expenses paid and a share in the proceeds when the book is published. The reason I put this in here is to put the record straight as to why I would do such a thing for someone I didn't really know, and to let you, the reader, know another facet of Bill Ford's character and personality – which is that he is a man of integrity who would never expect anything out of life that he couldn't pay for.

I have explored within myself the real question of, "Why I am doing this?" There has to be an over riding purpose beyond the normal reasons and motivation to start, maintain and complete a project of this magnitude in my spare time.

To put the task into context consider this: to achieve a doctorate of Philosophy, a PhD, which is the highest academic main stream achievement currently available in our society, it takes at least three years of research culminating in a thesis (a book) of at least 50,000 words. So I had to do the equivalent of a PhD in one year on my days off!

My purpose then: I wanted to know what has made a man such as Bill Ford, I wanted to bring his life to life and put it in such a way that the world can learn and know how he has done what he has. There's more satisfaction in giving than receiving, so it is said, so this is my gift to the world out there and it is part of my purpose to do the very best job that I can; and I now know, for sure, that I was one of the few people who could have done this for him.

The process of bringing this book to fruition has been the most satisfying work I have ever done – and, no matter what future reward may come, I am happy that it is a job well done and I am proud to present the story of a very rare fellow indeed.

From the outset Bill was adamant that we tell the truth, whether it be good or bad - but what we haven't done is tell the whole truth, nor have we told nothing but the truth. If we had done as one is asked in a court of law under oath, the detail would have swamped the story. We'd have ended up with lists of detail, like pieces of separate jigsaws which had no story to tell at all – a dossier of notes and maybe a scrapbook of memories and photos. So it has been my job to order these notes and create the story that hides within.

I have come to know my hero very well, so much so that I now consider him a true friend, the like of which I have never known before. True friends share secrets and therein lie some of the truths that won't ever be told. True friends share weaknesses and foibles of character, personality traits we'd rather do without - warts and all, so to speak. True friends are able to do this because a bond of trust develops that enables the truth to be told but not broadcasted. We achieved this and were then able to disseminate what the reader would like to know and more to the point, what they wouldn't.

At our first writing meeting, one of the first questions I asked Bill was this, "Who are you writing this book for?"

His answer came back immediately and was unequivocal, "For my family. In recent weeks and months, as I have spent time with Richard (Tilden Smith) I have realised that none of my family know much at all about my life. I've spent too much time away on business affairs and I'd like them to know me better."

In March 2017 Bill Ford was feeling almost friendless, that the whole pack of people that made up the Great Central Railway had dropped him like a stone - the very railway that he had fought so hard to rescue, to bring about its survival and subsequent prosperity and for purpose alone with no financial reward whatsoever. Worse than that, the board of directors, through Munro, had issued a statement saying that financial irregularities had been uncovered on Bill's watch. Her Majesty's Revenue and Customs department were to be informed, he would be implicated and he was not welcome on any part of railway property any longer. These allegations were of course fabricated, a device conjured up by Munro to get the board on his side and to reduce the "Bill Ford Effect" that Munro felt would undermine the building of his own regime.

There were days when Bill felt as if I was almost the only friend he had left who had anything to do with the GCR. I reassured him constantly that the "rank and file" felt the same as I did about him, holding him in high esteem. In September I invited him to our half yearly get together of "The Monday Crew" at The Waterside Inn in Mountsorrel, where we had the biggest turnout we'd ever had to come and say thank you to Bill.

We got through those dark days and came out the other end; now he knows there are only one or two he could consider as having acted malevolently towards him and he need never worry about not having a multitude of friends happy to see him anytime. Next to his family it is his friends he values most in his life. He has had wealth beyond which most of us could only ever dream, with possessions - houses, cars, boats and planes a plenty - but it is the people in his life that he cherishes beyond all else.

On one of our last writing meetings, we had lunch at The Horse and Hounds in Great Glen. For once I summoned up enough assertive resolve to get to pay the bill before he did! It was also the first time he had allowed me to drive him, too. He loves to drive and pay for lunch with equal desire. But only the week before he had spent another of his lives: he was driving home from an appointment in Market Harborough at a little after two in the afternoon, but remembers nothing more until he woke up in an ambulance. Debbie, who had been with him, was whisked off to hospital and made to stay over night before being allowed home. He still doesn't remember what happened and the poor old Mercedes was written off. Perhaps it was some sort of sign as his comment to me about the poor unfortunate dead car was, "I never liked the bloomin' thing anyway, it having once belonged to that Clive Baines!"

Clive Baines, a director of the GCR, is not one whom Bill has ever considered to be a friend...

It was yet another revelation to me to have Bill Ford as a passenger. He showed me where he'd had the accident the week before. He showed me the church where Claire is buried and the big house they were living in when she died in 1973. I was shown the house where Jane his daughter lives and the school where she teaches. I saw the new little cottage Bill and Debbie have bought and will move into this summer, their present house being rather too big for their needs these days.

We talked about Ford and Slater, how it still thrives to this day, the times in Africa, America and Saudi Arabia and how he felt that his years spent as a tax exile in the Isle of Man were a total waste of time. And as he looked out of the window onto this green - *his* green and pleasant land - I'm sure there was a tear in his eye.

When we first set out on this writing journey in March 2017, perhaps we should have begun by just driving around the countryside. He told more about his inner soul in that journey back to Kibworth than he had in a dozen mornings sitting at his kitchen table.

So, has my opinion of Bill Ford changed now that I know so much more about him? Of course it has! He is a man who has truly walked with kings, ne'er lost the common touch. But what he never does, never could do, is stoop to someone else's level. No, he brings you up to his height, shows you his world and lets you in.

Has he slipped from that pedestal where I placed him? Oh no, certainly not, I am up there with him now…

He told me a secret as we passed the church, one that I think I can share:

"I wasn't the best husband I could have been to Claire, you know… During the bad times in the life I've led I thought it was God punishing me. And I never thought I'd live past forty! On balance though, I have lived a charmed life I suppose…"

Throughout this journey Bill's wife, Debbie, has been with us every step of the way. Sometimes she was out at work, flying as a cabin crew member for the travel group *Tui*, but she always left things in order so Bill and I could carry on as we had left off the week before. Always thoughtful, she provided hot cross buns at Easter and biscuits at all times. If we had to work over a lunch time she would make the most delicious sandwiches - ham, cheese or smoked salmon and cake to follow. I remember one week when she went out shopping and left Bill and I to our work. It was after Bill told me about eating exotic fruits in Africa and I'd told him that I had never eaten paw-paw. Debbie brought some back for me and they are now a favourite. She has been a tremendous help with photo collecting, finding exactly the picture I was asking for and sending it through on an email within the hour. So, thank you Debbie, for looking after us and for your excellent illustrations when I realised we needed something a bit special in some parts of the book.

And finally, my biggest thanks go to Mary, my wife. She is the most diligent, tenacious and level headed person I know and we make a brilliant partnership. Her editing skills are second to none and if there are any errors remaining, which I doubt very much, they will be mine and mine alone - for having fiddled with the book after she has done her work! She has probably spent as many hours proofreading and editing this book as I have in writing it, such is the nature of producing a book of this type. One could almost say that the writing of it is the easy bit! So, thank you Mary, you are an absolute star!

As Bill alluded to in his afterword, this book is a shining example of teamwork - take anyone out of the project and the book would not be the best that it could be.

Now it is, and we all hope you think so too...

Steve Johns 31st March 2018

★   ★   ★

Credits for Photographs

No. 1 Ford Family Album
No. 2 Ford Family Album
No. 3 Ford Family Album
No. 4 Ford Family Album
No. 5 Ford Family Album
No. 6 Ford Family Album
No. 7 Ford Family Album
No. 8 Leicester Mercury
No. 9 Leicester Mercury
No. 10 Ford Family Album
No. 11 Ford Family Album
No. 12 Ford Family Album
No. 13 Ford Family Album
No. 14 Ford Family Album
No. 15 Ford Family Album
No. 16 Leicester Topic
No. 17 Google Earth
No. 18 Leicester Topic
No. 19 Leicester Topic
No. 20 Leicester Topic
No. 21 Ford Family Album
No. 22 Ford Family Album
No. 23 Ford Family Album
No. 24 Ford Family Album
No. 25 Ford Family Album
No. 26 Auto Vend
No. 27 Ford Family Album
No. 28 Ford Family Album
No. 29 Ford Family Album
No. 30 Ford Family Album
No. 31 Ford Family Album
No. 32 Ford Family Album
No. 33 Ford Family Album

Photo credits continued

No. 34 © Stowe School
No. 35 © Stowe School
No. 36 Ford Family Album
No. 37 Ford Family Album
No. 38 © Union Castle Archive
No. 39 © Memorable Meanders
No. 40. Ford Family Album
No. 40 Ford Family Album
No. 41 Ford Family Album
No. 42 Ford Family Album
No. 43 Ford Family Album
No. 44 © Steve Johns/ Lord Lanesborough Scrapbook
No. 45 Lord Lanesborough Scrapbook
No. 46 Lord Lanesborough Scrapbook
No. 47 © Graham Wignall
No. 48 © Graham Wignall
No. 49 © Graham Wignall
No. 50 © Graham Wignall
No. 51 © Graham Wignall
No. 52 © Graham Wignall
No. 53 © Graham Wignall
No. 54 © Graham Wignall
No. 55 © Graham Wignall
No. 56 © Graham Wignall
No. 57 © Graham Wignall
No. 58 Lord Lanesborough Scrapbook

Monochrome photographs on pages:
227 - Ford Family Album
275 - Lord Lanesborough Scrapbook
291 © Graham Wignall

Credits for Illustrations

Front cover - © Ian R Ward

On the following pages all credits to
© Richard Tilden Smith:
21: - Coventry Cathedral 1940
22: - 18 Marina Road, Leicester
27: - Stonebridge Street, Leicester
28: - Luftwaffe over Leicester
36: - Setting the school alight
56: - Blow Stowe!
67: - Racing The Flying Scotsman at East Fortune
68: - Head on
91: - The drive to the Stone House
94: - Arriving at Cape Town
103: - Storm in the Bay of Biscay
104: - Hello Big Boy
122: - Stuck in the Mud on Safari
143: - Leyland Albion beats Mercedes
158: - Up, Up and Away over Kilimanjaro.
180: - Clock Tower, Leicester
190: - Pa's Garage
212: - All Downhill at Foxton
252: - Flying from Manx
278: - A Loco with no name
292: - Leander On
310: - Leander Attacks Shap Summit
334: - ...and Goodnight

On the following pages all credits go to
© Debbie Ford
144: - Love's Labours Lost
224: - Forget Me Mot
242: - The Cuckoo

On the following page all credits go to
© Michael Gawer
336: - Line Drawing in Cantata Stoica 1955